Personalizing
Professional
Growth

D1240142

Personalizing Professional Growth

Staff Development That Works

Bernadette Marczely

CORWIN PRESS, INC.
A Sage Publications Company
Thousand Oaks, California

For information address:

Corwin Press, Inc.
A Sage Publications Company
2455 Teller Road
Thousand Oaks, California 91320
e-mail: order@corwin.sagepub.com

SAGE Publications Ltd.
6 Bonhill Street
London EC2A 4PU
United Kingdom

SAGE Publications India Pvt. Ltd.
M-32 Market
Greater Kailash I
New Delhi 110 048 India

Printed in the United States of America

Library of Congress Cataloging-in-Publication Data

Marczely, Bernadette.
    Personalizing professional growth : staff development that works /
by Bernadette Marczely.
        p.   cm.
    Includes bibliographical references and index.
    ISBN 0-8039-6433-1 (cloth : acid-free paper) . — ISBN
0-8039-6434-X (pbk. : acid-free paper)
        1. Teachers—In-service training—United States—Problems,
exercises, etc. 2. Teacher-administrator relationships—United
States.   I. Title.
LB1731.M34   1996
371.1′46—dc20   96-10056

This book is printed on acid-free paper.

96 97 98 99 00 10 9 8 7 6 5 4 3 2 1

Corwin Press Production Editor: S. Marlene Head

Contents

Preface

In our search to provide for the professional development of teachers, we have ignored two of the fundamental traits of a true professional: individuality and self-determination. Unlike doctors, lawyers, and other professionals, teachers are rarely given the opportunity to choose among a variety of professional development avenues. Professional development for educators has been defined as the process or processes by which minimally competent teachers achieve higher levels of professional competence and expand their understanding of self, role, context, and career (Duke & Stiggins, 1990), and with a lockstep determination public school staff development tends to assume that all teachers are at a level of minimal competence. Teachers, however, are not all at a level of minimum competence or, for that matter, at the same level of competence. There is no single teacher profile on which professional development can be based.

At present, the goal of professional development is usually pursued through a single recipe intended to satisfy all participants and all needs with one approach. With almost blind regimentation, school districts assess needs; seek speakers and experts to address these needs; conduct mandatory programs; evaluate speakers, experts, and programs; and return teachers compelled to attend these programs basically unchanged to their classrooms. In more than a century, no fundamental changes have been made in the way American teachers teach (Cuban, 1990; Warren, 1985). Principals, teachers, and other staff have responded to criticism of their schools by adding new programs and spending hours planning change, but despite these good intentions, we are beginning to realize how little they are changing what teachers do daily and thus what students learn (Sizer, 1992; Toch, 1991). Research shows that current staff development practices are inadequate to effect meaningful changes (Goldenberg & Gallimore, 1991). The reason, nevertheless, for this inadequacy has remained a mystery.

Perhaps, however, the underlying cause for the professional paralysis we now encounter is our inability to give teachers meaningful personal options and acknowledge that as professionals they must be allowed to select from a variety of professional development programs and approaches if real and lasting growth and change are to be achieved. Teachers are not all the same. An array of studies attests to varied stages of teacher growth and career development (Hange, 1982; Ingvarson & Greenway, 1981; Newman, Burden, & Applegate, 1980a, 1980b; Ryan et al., 1979). But professional development practice has, for the most part, ignored the need to get beyond blind prescriptive "training" in large-group settings and to personalize the professional development experience.

The ways in which educational leaders can work with teachers to personalize professional development plans will be explored in this book. It is written to help all educators become the architects of their own professional goals by identifying personal strengths, weaknesses, predispositions, and needs and designing professional growth programs that respond to these personal parameters.

This book will present ways in which a program of individualized professional development can be designed to function within the existing public school administrative and contractual structure. Eight distinct models for professional development will be discussed, with a ninth option combining approaches:

- Instruction-centered staff development
- Focused-training staff development
- Focused-research staff development
- Merit pay staff development
- School improvement staff development
- Internal career ladder staff development
- External career ladder staff development
- Self-directed staff development
- A combined approach

The models differ in their objectives, in the underlying assumptions on which each is based, and in the research and theory supporting each. Every approach is not suitable for every teacher, and each model places its own unique demands on the administrator involved. Therefore, profiles of the teacher and administrator most likely to succeed with each model are presented, and discussion questions accompany each approach to assist teachers and administrators in determining if they can be comfortable and successful in implementing a particular approach.

The underlying philosophical issues of each model, budget considerations, and accountability are also explored, and discussion questions encourage a closer examination of the potential issues and problems accompanying controversial approaches. Because field study is an important aspect of staff development planning, readers are given the opportunity to examine how each approach may function in their school settings. Activities intended to give students field experience in studying the effect of an approach in a real school setting follow each chapter. For example, students are asked to interview administrators and union leaders concerning the feasibility of an approach and their perception of obstacles and effectiveness. In addition, students are asked to plan for specific implementation of an approach in their unique settings. These exercises have the purpose of carrying research and theory presented into practice.

Planning guides are also provided for giving form and substance to the adoption of each model. They format basic questions that must be answered in pursuing a particular staff development approach, and they help define roles, responsibilities, and timelines. The guides are meant to do just that, guide teachers and administrators in their efforts to structure personalized professional growth plans. A subsequent chapter deals with how the products of the planning guides can be evaluated by using professional portfolios that record how specific goals and objectives have been met.

The book also discusses the roles of the superintendent, the professional staff developer, the principal, and the union in planning and implementing personalized professional growth programs. Professional qualifications, responsibilities, and personal accountability for each are addressed, and their interaction in planning and implementing a successful professional growth program is discussed.

Finally, the traditional obstacles to providing quality staff development are confronted. Because many of the approaches are new and controversial, every effort has been made to anticipate the potential problems and objections posed by their adoption. Organizational, management, fiscal, and collective bargaining obstacles are addressed, and suggestions for overcoming these obstacles are offered. In short, every effort is made to show how each model can be successfully implemented within the organizational, contractual, and fiscal realities of existing public schools. Specific ways to provide time, money, and support are given, and examples of working paradigms are cited where they exist. The intent of the book is to present a new delivery system for staff development in the context of existing organizational restraints, a system that will professionalize teaching by acknowledging the need for personalized professional growth.

BERNADETTE MARCZELY

About the Author

Bernadette Marczely is a Professor in the College of Education at Cleveland State University in Cleveland, Ohio. Before coming to Cleveland State, she served as a public school teacher, assistant principal, principal, and director of personnel. Presently, she is Director of the master's and certification programs in the area of supervision, and she is a licensed Ohio attorney practicing in the areas of school and employment law.

Special thanks to my husband David
for his technical and moral support

1

Looking at Other Professions

As we explore the reasons for the failure to implement effective and needed change in the field of education, we must again look at the profession of teaching in contrast to other professions. Law and medicine, unlike education, have made meaningful change a reality and an integral part of their disciplines. The plethora of medical advances extending both the quality and quantity of life and the evolving legal norms that change to reflect the changing needs of the society they serve are the products of the legal and medical communities' professional pursuit of meaningful change. They have progressed by encouraging personalized research, diversified training, and risk taking within their ranks. These professions offer their constituents a wide range of professional development alternatives from which to choose in structuring their careers. A doctor, for example, can be a general practitioner, specialist, researcher, writer, consultant, or teacher, or engage in any combination of those roles throughout a career. Similarly, a lawyer may generalize or limit a law practice but may also write, research, mediate or arbitrate disputes, consult or teach in interest areas, or combine these avenues of practice. One need not abandon the basic calling in order to move freely from one interest area to the next in these professions. One's only real limits are personal choice and commitment. If one is willing and able to take on new challenges, relatively few obstacles to success and professional respect appear along the way.

In education, in contrast, risk taking, experimentation, and movement within the professional ranks has never been encouraged and is often actually discouraged. Traditionally, teachers have been classroom practitioners deeply involved in the everyday realities of their work, and in this role they are subject to the deadening effects of routine (Rudduck, 1989). Schools, themselves lulled by a perceived need for regimentation, do not traditionally accommodate experimentation. Schools, like the teachers within them, have come to accept and, in fact, cultivate an enervating status quo that discourages meaningful risk taking and change for the system as well as the individual.

In addition, education is a decidedly stratified profession. Practicing teachers are not encouraged to be writers, researchers, or innovators, and their rare sorties into these areas are greeted with skepticism and cynical dismissal. The published treatises on how to teach effectively are rarely written by practicing classroom teachers. They are written by those who have left the public school classroom. They are sometimes even written by those who have never taught in a public school classroom.

Whereas doctors and lawyers seldom assign credence to treatises in their fields written by nonpractitioners, educators embrace the theories, critiques, and opinions of those outside the classroom. There is a traditional deference to the musings of nonpractitioners in the field of education. Practicing teachers do not write the books intended for either preservice or inservice instruction, nor does the lockstep system that frames their careers give them the time, incentive, or support to do so. As a result, field practitioners too often succumb to the professional inertia euphemistically termed *burnout*, and neophytes to the classroom are trained by those who do not actually practice what they preach. The end result is devastating for individual teachers, neophytes and veterans, as well as for the profession. Actual teaching experience is subliminally devalued, and classroom teaching becomes a professional cul-de-sac.

How Change Can Be Created

Change in behavior is brought about by four basic learning conditions: stimulus, response, reinforcement, and motivation (Rebore, 1991). Our present approach to staff development, however, neglects the motivation factor. To be truly effective in what they do, teachers must rise above the status of Pavlov's dogs locked in a training cycle that attends only to stimulus, response, and reinforcement. Teachers must believe they will affect and be directly affected by the programs in which they are asked to participate and that they have independently chosen to participate. This is far more likely to happen when individual teachers, like other professionals, are allowed to pursue programs tailored to their individual needs and are given viable and challenging options from which to choose.

The career cycle of a teacher is not a linear progression from preservice to exit. Fessler and Christensen (1992) described a teacher's career cycle as a dynamic ebb and flow, with teachers moving in and out of career stages in response to environmental influences from both the personal and organizational dimensions. Figure 1.1 illustrates some of the significant factors in teachers' personal, professional, and organizational lives that may affect their response to professional development. Like concentric wheels of fortune spun independently of each other by time and circumstance, these factors can line up in varying combinations for maximum effect. The wheels keep turning as factors in each arena rise and fall in importance to the individual, and the only constant that can be planned for is the inevitable change.

As Figure 1.1 indicates, there are myriad ways that factors can combine to create unique teacher profiles. The two profile circles at the bottom of the figure show how differently two teachers in the same school may be affected by factors in their personal, professional, and organizational lives. Profile Circle A represents a nontenured elementary teacher with a family of four to support. Profile Circle B is that of a tenured high school teacher with no dependents. Their professional development needs will be decidedly different. Teacher A will have a need to teach well and complete the graduate studies required to earn tenure and a secure professional future. In contrast, Teacher B may be ready, willing, and able to take the risks required by new professional challenges. Their needs differ and so, too, should their professional growth opportunities and challenges. They will each be motivated by different factors, and no single staff development program will satisfy both. Staff development planners must not neglect the very different factors motivating each.

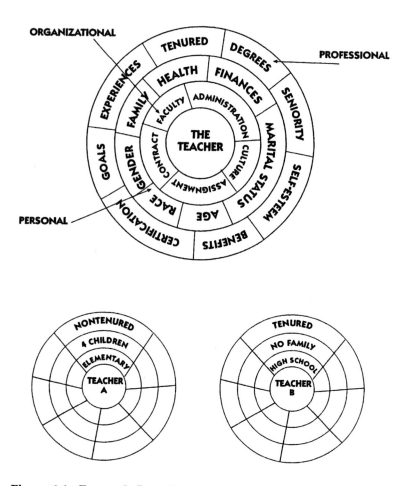

Figure 1.1. Factors Influencing Teacher Professional Development Profiles

The Security Factor

Under our present system, teaching is a relatively secure profession and, as such, provides few incentives for growth or change. To reject the status quo is to sacrifice the security promised by the present system. Participation in programs for improving teaching skills or restructuring the way things are presently done are often viewed as a threat to the security of the status quo, an admission that all is not well in the first place. Thus the organization itself often impedes meaningful professional growth by perpetuating an environment that discourages the risk taking required for change.

The traditional management style of some district and building administrators in a similar manner works to inhibit growth. Teachers must have time, support, and understanding to deal with their professional goals, yet many educational managers run schools with an assembly line mentality that ignores the need for professional reflection. They, too, are comfortable with the way things are and reluctant to give teachers time out of the classroom "harness" to deal with a big picture that has not been generically defined.

Last, society itself often impedes the professional growth of teachers by questioning its economic value. The concepts of research and development are viewed as foreign to the field of education. Uninformed parents and board members sometimes actually see teacher development programs as an interruption in the learning process. They expect teachers to be in their classrooms every day. In essence, the public tends to view its teachers as glorified baby-sitters, and the expenditure of funds for professional growth that takes them out of the classroom as a breach of the public trust and a waste of money.

These attitudes, together with an unwillingness to treat teachers as unique professionals, create the career frustration and debilitating inertia that thwart attempts at meaningful change in the field of education. Each teacher is affected by a unique combination of personal, organizational, and professional factors that form the context in which professional development must take place. Meaningful change begins with the individual. Thus it should be obvious that no single plan for professional growth can respond to the needs of all or even many teachers. It should also be obvious when we look to other professions that personalized research and development is the key to professional progress for both the individual and the organization. Teachers who feel professionally fulfilled will generate the programs, procedures, and research that create successful schools. However, relinquishing the status quo will not be easy. It will require the development of professional trust among all affected parties.

Discussion Questions

1. Interview a teacher who has left the classroom concerning the reasons for that career choice. Would the teacher have preferred to remain in the classroom?

2. Interview a member of another profession about professional growth programs available within that profession. Do these differ from those available to teachers?

3. In a group, discuss future career goals. Where do you see yourself 5 years from now? Where do you see yourself 10 years from now?

4. Discuss how your school presently handles professional development for teachers. Have the district's programs been effective? Why or why not?

5. Using Figure 1.1 as a guide, describe those factors that have had a significant effect on you within the past year. Compare your response with that of a colleague, and discuss how these factors influence your professional growth needs at this point in time.

2

Adult Learning and Effective Staff Development

Knox (1986) noted that effective adult learning is an active search for meaning where content and personal experience are blended. The concerns-based adoption model (CBAM), a program developed at the Texas Research and Development Center for Teacher Education, studied what happens to individuals when they try out new practices or implement innovations (Hall, Loucks, Rutherford, & Newlove, 1975). A basic tenet of this model is that people are most concerned about how changes affect them personally. With this research in mind, good staff development must consider the goals of individual teachers as well as those of the school and district and work to integrate these into a whole (Loucks-Horsley et al., 1987). Effective staff development must be grounded in the mundane but very real details of teachers' daily work lives, but in a form that provides the intellectual stimulation of a graduate seminar (Goldenberg & Gallimore, 1991). That is, effective staff development must engage teachers in a sustained analysis of teaching as a professional pursuit (Goldenberg & Gallimore, 1991). Such personal engagement begins with acknowledging the individuality of teachers and creating a staff development format that responds to this individuality.

It is this concern for the individual that is sorely lacking in present professional development planning. Unlike other professions, education gives teachers few personal options when it comes to professional development. Too much of what we presently do is collective inservice, not personalized professional development. Inservice education is oriented toward immediate collective training objectives, whereas professional development implies engagement in persistent and personally significant activities (Orlich, 1989). A successful professional development program should be characterized by diversity of ideas, people, and support practices (Loucks-Horsley et al., 1987). Options must be made available, with the only prescription being that the teacher take the time to establish personal, professional goals and choose options that will help to attain them. In successful staff development, teachers are active participants rather than passive reactors. They have an identified personal interest in the program they pursue and are therefore motivated to achieve the goals they set.

Successful teachers do this every day for their students. Teachers integrate a variety of instructional strategies in their classrooms, recognizing that no single strategy works best at all times for all students (Guskey, 1990). Schools must come to recognize that the same need for individualization exists in professional development for teachers themselves. Teachers differ, not only in the professional goals they set for themselves but also in their learning modes, stages of development, philosophies, and abilities.

Joyce and McKibbin (1982) found that teachers in the same school responded differently to the same opportunities for professional growth and identified five growth stages to try to explain the differences:

1. *Omnivores:* Teachers who actively use every available aspect of the formal and informal systems that are available to them.

2. *Active consumers:* Teachers who take advantage of many (but not all) opportunities for growth and who occasionally initiate activities.

3. *Passive consumers:* Teachers who are there when opportunity presents itself but who rarely seek or initiate new activities.

4. *Reticents:* Teachers who are unlikely to seek out training (or challenges) unless it is in areas in which they already feel successful.

5. *Withdrawns:* Teachers who avoid virtually all growth-oriented activity.

Effective professional development anticipates this diversity and accommodates it in philosophy, method, and evaluation.

Ultimately, there is strength in diversity, a strength that to date has been untapped in education. Our present approach to professional growth has all teachers marching to the monotonous beat of a single drummer while an orchestra waits in the wings.

How Adults Learn

Malcolm Knowles (1984, 1986) assumed adult learners have a great degree of self-directedness, have experiences that form a knowledge base, and learn by solving problems. Successful staff development acknowledges that adults need choices and that a training workshop is only one strategy (Hirsh & Ponder, 1991). The staff development approaches presented in this book provide the choice Knowles's profile of the adult learner demands.

Knowles's assumptions have important implications for those who plan and direct staff development programs:

1. Adults enjoy planning and conducting their own learning experiences.
2. Experiences are key to self-actualization.
3. The best learning takes place when need to know coincides with the training.
4. Adults need opportunities to apply what they have learned.
5. Adults need some independent structured options (Orlich, 1989).

These assumptions provide the philosophical foundation for the proposed models for personalized professional growth. Each of the approaches is discussed with respect to how it will affect individual professional development. Professionalism is synonymous with growth and improvement rather than the change-for-the-sake-of-change philosophy that too often fuels staff development. There is no reason to insist on "constant change"; rather, the focus should be on the Japanese notion of *kaizen* or "constant improvement" (Raebeck, 1994). Improvement, however, is a unique measurement because it must begin with the individual teacher and that individual teacher's present professional status. It is on the present that plans for future improvement must be laid. Improvement is a personal mission that begins with self-appraisal and is spurred on by the promise of something better in the end. Asking people to do anything that they do not feel has at least a good chance of leading to something better is asking too much (Raebeck, 1994). Thus it becomes important for those who plan professional development programs to know teachers as individuals and to work with them to plan for both personal and organizational improvement.

The Nexus Between School Improvement and Personal Growth

This approach does not subjugate the needs of the school to the needs of the individual; rather, it sees the two as inextricably entwined and interdependent. Today, accountability demands require that influence on student outcomes be a principal focus in evaluating staff development programs (Guskey & Sparks, 1991a). Schools, however, will improve only when the teachers in them improve methods, means, and mindsets. Therefore, the central focus of staff development must begin with the individual teacher but will ultimately relate back to improvement in the learning process and in student achievement.

Teachers who feel professionally unfulfilled and trapped impede student achievement either directly or indirectly. Teacher burnout has been the term coined to describe the emotional and intellectual capitulation of a professional without options. But meaningful personal change embodied in real career choices for teachers can give new hope directly to teachers and indirectly to the children they serve. Such an approach can give rise to a wellspring of creativity and commitment to achievement not presently found in public education.

The approaches presented in this book strive to provide meaningful options for teachers that will positively affect student performance. The instruction-centered, focused-training, focused-research, and merit pay models for staff development all are directly related to improving immediate classroom performance. The school improvement and internal career ladder models focus on improving student performance in the expanded schoolwide or district setting. The external career ladder model takes this movement beyond the classroom one step further by giving the teacher an opportunity to perform in roles totally outside of the classroom and the immediate school district. In doing so, this model may appear to have no relationship to the immediate classroom. Nevertheless, the external career ladder model has a very important indirect effect on the learning environment. This model offers new avenues for professional growth that may ultimately have a profound effect on all aspects of the educational environment. This model will dispel forever the public perception that "those who can't do, teach." The external career ladder also brings a new freedom to teachers who wonder what might have been had they opted for careers in the real world. It gives them opportunities beyond the traditional classroom door and the contractual pay scale—a chance to explore career change within the context of education without leaving the field or completely severing the tie to the classroom. It answers the question "What might have been?" in a productive new way that is beneficial to teacher, district, school, and student.

3

Instruction-Centered
Staff Development

The vast majority of teachers are happy teaching and take pride in what they do. They are devoted to their students and want only to improve what they are presently doing in the classroom, that is, to make learning more appealing and effective. The problem is that teachers have relatively little time or incentive to examine and assess their own performance and to review the array of strategies that promise to improve that performance. They also have virtually no freedom to select the course of study or training they might believe best addresses their needs in the classroom. Strategies for improving classroom performance and student achievement are selected *for* teachers not *by* teachers. That selection may be made by the school or district administration or by a committee of other teachers, but the individual teacher has no ultimate control over the selection. For both philosophical and economic reasons, strategies for improvement are rarely selected by individual teachers. Economically, districts want staff development programs to reach large audiences. Philosophically, district administrations want consistency in teaching practice and outcome and believe that the way to attain this goal is to provide uniform training for teachers. Ignoring teacher individuality, however, may actually result in a resistance on the part of teachers that ultimately undermines both these goals. Individual needs and concerns are lost in large-group instruction thereby defeating its purpose.

The instruction-centered model for professional growth is designed to give teachers an opportunity to reflect on a variety of teaching styles and on what works and what does not work for them as individuals. The model is designed to give them the time and encouragement to evaluate what they are presently doing and try out new theories and approaches that might improve classroom performance, to adopt those that prove successful, and to discard those that do not.

The model differs from traditional supervision and evaluation approaches in that the teacher, with or without the help of an administrator, plans and conducts the procedures for implementing the model. Assessment of present practice is the first step in the process and can be done by videotaping one's own performance, having a peer assess performance, or working directly with an administrator in a traditional mode. This process, however, is not traditional evaluation with job security implications. Rather, it is the teacher professional personally examining ways to improve teaching skills and effectiveness.

The assessment is planned around the collection and analysis of data gathered during a lesson in order to diminish the effect of subjectivity and personal confrontation. This is an objective professional learning exercise, not the tedious show-and-tell ritual of traditional observation and evaluation. With this goal in mind, the teacher may self-videotape or -audiotape, or work with peer or principal in a planned program of data collection and analysis. The instruction-centered model's focus is teacher and student performance in the classroom. Teachers are observed in the process of teaching, data are collected during the observation, and the data are analyzed and discussed by the teacher and with the teacher. Through this process of observation and feedback, the teacher examines, reflects on, and plans to improve classroom performance.

The collection and analysis of data should ideally involve clinical supervision techniques such as verbatim or selective verbatim scripting, verbal flow charts, at-task analysis, interactional analysis, and anecdotal descriptions of what is happening in the classroom (Acheson & Gall, 1992). By these methods, the observer can objectively record data reflecting what is happening in the classroom and by means of that data assess the effectiveness of the learning environment. Ideally, the teacher selects both the observer and the mode of observation, or collaborates with the observer on that selection. This stage of the model allows the teacher and observer to jointly and independently diagnose problems and plan for improving effectiveness.

The model is based on the premise that teaching can be objectively observed and analyzed and that improvement in teaching can result from feedback on that performance (Sparks & Loucks-Horsley, 1990). It also assumes that reflection and analysis are central means of professional growth (Loucks-Horsley et al., 1987). This professional growth opportunity is actually shared by the teacher observed and the observer. The teacher benefits by another's view of the teaching behavior and the resultant feedback; the observer benefits by observing a colleague, preparing the feedback, and discussing the common experience (Sparks & Loucks-Horsley, 1990). Together, they work as professionals analyzing what they do and working to improve what they do, and the resultant plan is personalized for optimum results.

The instruction-centered model has its roots in *effective teaching research*. This research has produced a pattern of instruction that is particularly useful in teaching a body of well-defined skills (Rosenshine, 1986). Ned Flanders (1970) identified contrasting styles of teaching. Barak Rosenshine and Norma Furst (1973) identified nine characteristics of teachers whose students make greater gains in academic achievement than students of other teachers. And in 1984, Madeline Hunter published her "instructional theory into practice" model's seven components for effective classroom teaching, a parallel to Rosenshine's (1986) "explicit teaching model." Each has essentially found that technique in the classroom affects learning and that feedback contrasting what is with what should be is vital to improving classroom performance on the part of both teachers and students.

Bloom (1956) referred to critique as part of evaluation, the highest order of thinking, and the instruction-centered model is based on the theory that objective critique of classroom performance is the path to true professional self-improvement. Proponents of this model also believe individual teachers are unlikely to be motivated to grow without the feedback of peers, supervisors, students, or parents providing the challenge found to be vital to stage growth (movement from one developmental level to another) (Thies-Sprinthall & Sprinthall, 1987).

Contractual Concerns

To be a true learning experience, the teacher must be free to discover what does not work as well as what does without the threat to self-esteem and position security associated with a traditional poor evaluation. If the observer is an administrator, it may be difficult to dissociate this model from traditional evaluation. The role of the administrator as one with power to hire, fire, promote, and assign may cast a threatening pall on the experience. Yet contract and board policy may require that an administrator play a central role in the assessment of classroom performance. Thus it becomes essential to distinguish use of the instruction-centered model for professional development from contractual evaluation. Effective staff development cannot take place in a potentially punitive atmosphere. There must be freedom to err and try again if true learning is to take place.

Peer coaching programs are an alternative method for implementing this model in a way that moves it out of the shadow of evaluative control and into the light of professional development. There is evidence that peers, as well as administrators, can play a key role in growth-oriented teacher evaluation (Glatthorn, 1987; D. W. Johnson & Johnson, 1987). Garmston (1987) noted that peer coaching enhances collegiality, creates occasions for professional dialogue, and allows teachers to develop a vocabulary about instruction. In either case, use of clinical supervision techniques in observing and conferencing can increase the objectivity and collegiality needed to make this model work with both administrator and peer observers.

Objectivity and shared professional concern are the watchwords of this approach. So much of what happens under present evaluation systems is indeed just ritualized show-and-tell underscored by the need to establish job security. Teachers are at best observed once a year, and feedback is minimal and easily dismissed. Teachers themselves often view the process as required administrative ritual rather than a professional development opportunity. Observations under the instruction-centered model, in contrast, occur repeatedly, and there is follow-up to the initial critique. Suggestions for improvement are discussed, implemented, and evaluated regularly.

Teacher and Administrator Profile

The teacher best served by this staff development model varies. Obviously, the teacher experiencing problems with instructional organization and classroom management can be helped to improve with this model. New and inexperienced teachers, in particular, will benefit from consultation with an experienced professional mentor.

They will learn the vocabulary of teaching. They will also be taught the art of professional reflection and objective discussion of their craft.

Teachers at other levels of experience and expertise, however, may also benefit from using this model. Teachers who sense problems in the classroom may use the clinical supervision and consultation techniques of the model to confirm or dispel their fears and plan for more effective learning. In addition, experienced and proficient teachers, with no immediate concerns, may profit from this approach to professional reflection and growth. Even good teaching must be examined from time to time and often can be improved. In other words, there need not be a problem to initiate participation in instruction-centered staff development.

As with each of the models presented, however, effectiveness will depend on the personal traits and goals of the teacher and the building administrator. Figure 3.1 indicates the teacher and administrator personality traits that will have an effect on the effectiveness of this model.

Response to criticism is a pivotal factor in determining if this model is right for a given teacher. Teachers who withdraw in the face of constructive criticism may find this model intimidating until they have developed the self-confidence that comes with experience. This model will also have only a marginal effect on jaded veterans who do not value the opinion of others. Introspection and an openness to new ideas are needed to facilitate use of this model.

Administrators must also have an inherent faith in the value of constructive criticism for this model to succeed. The administrator must be an informed and respected resource, one who facilitates the model's implementation by providing time and encouragement. This model will only succeed in schools where the ongoing study of the teaching craft is indigenous to the culture.

Personal assessment questions follow to assist teachers and building administrators in determining if this model can be effective for them. The questions will also sensitize teachers and administrators to the emotional pitfalls and obstacles.

Ten Questions for Teachers

1. Do you regularly examine what you do in the classroom?
2. Do you welcome constructive criticism?

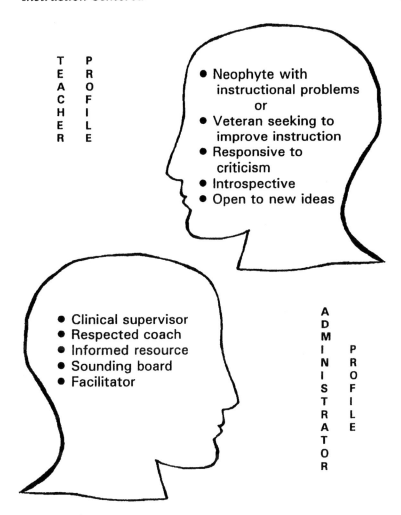

Figure 3.1. Instruction-Centered Staff Development Model

3. Do you sense problems with your performance as a teacher?

4. When have you last done something differently at the suggestion of another?

5. Do you believe that your performance as a teacher can be improved?

6. Do you value the opinions of your peers?

7. How do you feel when you are observed in the process of teaching?
8. How often have you been observed by a teacher or administrator?
9. Is there a new teaching technique you have wanted to try?
10. Do you believe you are a good teacher?

Ten Questions for Administrators

1. Do you believe you can help teachers improve their performance?
2. Ideally, how often should an administrator visit each teacher?
3. Are you familiar with the techniques of clinical supervision?
4. What is the most important aspect of your work as an administrator?
5. How often do you presently observe each teacher in your building?
6. What obstacles do you anticipate in implementing this model?
7. Do you believe you were or are an effective teacher?
8. Do you feel teachers under your supervision respect you?
9. Do you believe there are ways to improve teacher performance?
10. How can you overcome the obstacles to implementing this model?

The Method

Implementation of this model relies on the methods of clinical supervision and on such concepts as "cognitive coaching" and the "critical friend" for successful implementation. The cognitive coach uses the preconference, observation, and postconference of clinical supervision for the sole purpose of helping the teacher improve instructional effectiveness by becoming more reflective about teaching (Garmston, Linder, & Whitaker, 1993). The ultimate goal of cognitive coaching is teacher autonomy: the ability to self-monitor, self-analyze, and self-evaluate (Garmston et al., 1993). A critical

Classroom focus:
Clinical supervisor or peer:
Data collection plan:
Data analysis:
Conclusions and suggestions for improvement:

Figure 3.2. Instruction-Centered Staff Development Planning Guide

friend, as the name suggests, is a trusted person who asks provocative questions, provides data to be examined through another lens, and offers a critique of a person's work as a friend (Costa & Kallick, 1993). Both the cognitive coach and the critical friend collect objective data to assist in initiating the reflective discussion central to this model.

Figure 3.2 provides a form for assisting teachers and their coaches in planning for instruction-centered staff development. This outline requires the delineation of the details of a plan for implementing the model.

Pros and Cons

There are those who would hold that every form of professional development must be student oriented. One of the most formidable arguments favoring the instruction-centered model is that it does focus on performance in the classroom. The model advocates the formative assessment of teaching practice as an avenue for professional growth and improvement of instruction. Both the National Education Association and the American Federation of Teachers have endorsed the use of teacher evaluation for formative purposes (Duke & Stiggins, 1990).

The model, by its very nature, acknowledges the importance of what goes on in the classroom and casts the teacher as a proactive catalyst for the success or failure of the learning process. The individual teacher, not the generic category "teacher," is the central focus of this model. Thus the model empowers individual teachers and enhances their professional self-esteem in contrast to models that cast them as part of a nebulous reactive group of deficient practitioners.

Those who would challenge the model's effectiveness, however, would say it cannot be divorced from raw accountability. This professional development model supports the collection and analysis of data in its quest to improve instruction. This same data can also be used to assess teacher performance in the classroom. It is the model's potential dual purpose that critics feel taints its effectiveness. The evaluation component prevents the very climate essential for learning and growth, that of experimentation and permission to fail, revision and trying again, while continuing to practice new but still awkward skills and procedures (Joyce & Showers, 1988).

No matter how well designed the evaluation system and how ample the support from supervisors and peers, teachers are unlikely to experience professional development if they are unable or unwilling to take advantage of opportunities for growth (Duke & Stiggins, 1990). Orientation to risk taking, openness to change, willingness to experiment, and openness to criticism have been linked to professional development success (Stiggins & Duke, 1988). Naysayers believe the evaluative character of the model inhibits the development of these characteristics in the teachers who may need assistance most.

Another criticism of the model centers on the time commitment required for effective implementation. Although few would dispute the benefit of performance feedback, those familiar with the hectic pace of schools resurrect the argument that finding time for providing quality feedback is difficult (Duke & Stiggins, 1990). At least two or more preconferences, observations, and conferences are required for this model to have its intended effect, and time for training peers and administrators in clinical supervision techniques cannot be discounted. Critics argue that such time commitment is impossible for peers as well as for administrators.

Administrators and teachers who choose to use this model as their professional growth plan should begin by discussing the pros and cons of this approach and how they may minimize potential problems. The following discussion questions address these issues and ask prospective participants to justify use of the model and plan for the time and resource commitment entailed.

Discussion Questions

1. Discuss arguments favoring the time commitment required by this model. Why should this model, with its inherent drawbacks, be used in professional development?
2. Brainstorm ways to assure that teachers and administrators have the time to successfully implement this model.
3. How would you evaluate the effectiveness of this model, and how can you structure procedures used to distinguish this model from traditional evaluation of teachers?
4. What is the most effective way to train teachers and administrators to use this model?
5. What are the contractual implications of using this model, and how are they best addressed?

As with each of the models presented, instruction-centered staff development is not right for every teacher or every administrator. This model works best for teachers and administrators who share a collegial trust and a belief that clinical supervision can improve instruction. It also works best in a district willing to make the required time and fiscal commitment to training in clinical supervision techniques and prescriptive conferencing. The teacher must see a purpose to the process, and the administrator must have the knowledge, sensitivity, and commitment to support the effort.

Field activities follow to give students experience in implementing the various aspects of this model in a real school setting. They are asked to implement some of the model's procedures and to react to their field effectiveness.

Activities

1. Ask a peer to observe you teaching a class and look for one way in which you can improve your performance as a teacher.

2. a. Review clinical techniques for observing classroom instruction (Acheson & Gall, 1992). Select one method to collect data on your own instructional performance, and ask a colleague to use this method to collect data that you can then use in analyzing your performance.

   b. Analyze the data collected, and use your analysis to suggest ways in which you can improve your teaching performance.

   c. Compare your conclusions with those of the colleague who has collected the data, and discuss your results.

3. Videotape one of your lessons and then analyze your performance.

4. Audiotape one of your lessons and then analyze your performance.

5. Explore ways of improving classroom instruction discussed in one of the published journals and then analyze your own classroom performance in light of this suggested method for improving instruction.

6. a. Ask a colleague whose work you admire if you can observe his or her class.

   b. Analyze procedures and approaches that appear to be particularly effective.

   c. Try one of these approaches in your own teaching and analyze effectiveness.

7. Read about, implement, and evaluate the effectiveness of one of these strategies: "wait time," "teacher expectations and student achievement," "mnemonics."

4

Focused-Training Staff Development

In the minds of many administrators and teachers, staff development is synonymous with training. Training is the process of learning a sequence of programmed behaviors (S. P. Robbins, 1982). Unlike the other models to be discussed, training focuses on the sequence of behaviors to be learned rather than on the learner. It is methodology centered and presumes that there is universal value and appeal in the behavior to be learned. The focused-training model assumes that there are a great many research-based effective teaching practices that have been identified and verified in the past 20 years that will improve the quality of classroom teaching (Sparks, 1983). This model also assumes that teachers *can* change their behaviors and learn to replicate behaviors in their classrooms that were not previously in their repertoire (Sparks & Loucks-Horsley, 1990). Finally, the model assumes that all teachers will accept the validity and applicability of the practice presented. Some see this model as a means of bridging the gap between research and practice in that it trains teachers to use the methods researchers have found to be particularly effective in the classroom.

Joyce and Showers (1988) have conducted significant research in training, and they describe training content in terms of three overlapping components:

1. Academic content
2. Curriculum and instructional strategies
3. School improvement processes

All training falls into one or more of these three categories. Academic content training is obviously directed at extending teacher knowledge in a subject area. Workshops to develop computer skills to be used in teaching math or in directing historical research would be an example of academic training. Curriculum and instructional strategy training, on the other hand, would present teachers with new ways to organize and teach the material to be learned. Inservices dealing with the whole language approach to teaching reading, or a problem-solving mathematics curriculum, illustrate this type of training. In contrast, training directed at changing attitudes and examining relationships is directed at school environment improvement. Assertive discipline training, cooperative learning, and self-esteem-building training programs are examples of this type of staff development.

Training should give opportunities for theory and practice to meet. Planned follow-up and maintenance activities are an integral part of effective training (F. Wood, 1989). Research in the area of training (Bennett, 1987; Joyce & Showers, 1988) identifies specific training components that appear to directly affect teachers' adoption and use of an innovation presented during training:

1. Presentation of theory
2. Modeling or demonstration
3. Practice under simulated conditions
4. Structured and open-ended feedback
5. Coaching for application

For training to be effective, all of these components must be part of the training program. This requires time and commitment on the part of those involved in planning, implementing, maintaining, and evaluating.

To bring a teaching model of medium complexity under control requires 20 or 25 trials in the classroom over a period of about 8 or 10 weeks (Joyce & Showers, 1988). Specific and nonevaluative feedback should take place as soon as possible following practice for optimum effect (Joyce & Showers, 1988). To assure that this happens, arrangements should be made for teachers to monitor other teachers applying new techniques in the classroom. Coaching is this technical feedback on the congruence of practice trials with ideal performance and is designed to follow up training inservice and help teachers perfect and maintain skills learned.

Other factors have also been found to affect teacher use of training. Doyle and Ponder (1977) suggest that three aspects of the manner in which an innovation is presented to teachers will affect their decision to use it:

- Instrumentality—how clearly and specifically new practices are presented
- Congruence—alignment of new practice with present philosophy and practice
- Cost—teachers' estimates of time and effort required compared to benefits promised

Perceived administrative support will also affect teacher use of training. Because changes in teacher attitudes and beliefs occur mainly after implementation takes place and evidence of improved student learning is gained, continued support following initial training is crucial (Guskey, 1986).

Planning for Training

Actual planning for training inservice entails eight steps:

1. Assessing needs
2. Reviewing programs addressing needs
3. Assessing costs and benefits of applicable programs
4. Developing a contract for services
5. Scheduling and advertising the inservice
6. Preparing the inservice site
7. Evaluating the inservice
8. Monitoring maintenance and effect

Assessing Needs

Research and experience suggest that it is best to involve teachers in planning training programs to give them a vested interest in the success of the programs. This involvement should begin with identifying the need for training. Needs assessment can be undertaken in a variety of ways, the most obvious being surveys, questionnaires, and interviews. Specific, already-identified problems within a school may also dictate need, as well as legislative mandates bearing on educational issues. Regardless of the strategy undertaken, or the source dictating the need, however, refined feedback should be a component of the needs assessment process. That is, teachers participating should be aware of how need is being determined, and they should be informed of the results of the needs assessment process so that the perception of arbitrary administrative topic selection is dispelled.

The Delphi technique is one way to identify organizational consensus, determine problem areas, and establish priorities by giving detailed feedback and systematic follow-up. The Delphi technique was developed and popularized by the RAND Corporation (Helmer, 1967). This technique involves participants in rounds of response and feedback, with each round narrowing and refining assessed needs. Respondents are an integral part of the process, and the responding group is constantly aware of how and why the process is narrowing selection. That is, at the end of each round, participants are told how many respondents viewed each given topic as important. This process takes time but is essential to having teachers feel commitment to the program finally undertaken.

Program Review and Selection

Once need is identified, the process of reviewing programs that address the identified need begins. Figure 4.1 lists sample inservice topics under subject area, curriculum and instructional strategies, and school improvement processes that may respond to identified needs in these areas. This list includes topics generated by state or federal government mandates—topics such as inclusion and the Goals 2000.

An important next step in implementing this model is actually previewing the programs available that address identified needs. Not all programs, presenters, materials, or costs are the same. Those planning for training must know the audience to be served and seek the best speaker and program for that audience and topic. Professional journals, through paid advertising and the articles published, can provide a starting point. In addition, presentations at professional

Subject Area Staff Development	Curriculum/ Instruction Strategies	School Improvement Strategies
Developmental reading	Cooperative learning	Building self-esteem
Critical thinking skills	Designing curriculum	Multiculturalism
Whole language reading	Learning dimensions	Sexual harassment in the schools
Phonics and reading	Learning styles	Special education in the 1990s
Linguistics	The Hunter model	Conflict resolution
Minority history	Outcome-based education	School law
Problem solving	Using technology	Communication skills
Geography revisited	Grouping for learning	Stress management
The new social studies	Portfolio assessment	Involving parents
Integrating curriculum	Brain research	Research review
Hands-on math	The middle school	Effective schools
Hands-on science	Developing activities	Shared decisions
Computer enrichment	Using audiovisuals	Assertive discipline
The liberal arts	Alternative education	Cooperative discipline
The Learning Center	Planning field trips	Teaching values
Life skills learning	Inclusion strategies	Public relations
Individualization	Evaluating the curriculum	Conferencing skills
Integrating science and mathematics	Selecting textbooks	Crisis intervention
	Evaluating assessment	

Figure 4.1. Inservice Topics

society meetings or commercial tapes developed by groups such as Phi Delta Kappa, the Association for Supervision and Curriculum Development, and various subject area societies give planners an idea of the range of research and rhetoric on any given topic. Careful planning begins with a thorough research review.

It is wise when selecting programs to review at least three that appear to address identified needs and compare the ways in which the following factors are addressed by each program:

- Underlying philosophy
- Supporting research
- Program activities
- Program materials
- Program maintenance activities

An inservice dealing with school discipline illustrates how significantly inservice programs can differ with respect to these factors. Canter and Canter's (1989) assertive discipline, Albert's (1989) cooperative discipline, and Canfield's (1986) self-esteem building all deal with ways that school districts can train teachers to minimize discipline problems in the classroom. All three, however, differ significantly with respect to the listed factors. A school striving for a consistently effective approach to discipline should review all three in light of its own philosophy and ability to adapt to the procedures and activities required. If teachers cannot identify with the philosophy presented, or find the procedures espoused cumbersome or affected, it is unlikely that the program can be effectively adopted. Thus comparative research and discussion become a vital part of inservice planning.

Program and presenter reference checks should also be an integral part of inservice selection. An opportunity to either hear or see a presenter in action can be an even better way to predict effectiveness. There are many fine writers who are simply not effective speakers, and there are many effective speakers whose approach to presentation may simply not be right for a particular group. At one devastating inservice, the presenter tried for humorous inspiration by telling one age-related joke after another to a veteran faculty with an average age of 50. Needless to say, many were put off and even insulted by the presenter's approach. They tuned out the inservice before it had even begun.

Planning committees must never forget that public funds are expended both directly and indirectly in implementing a training inservice, and fiscal accountability for teacher time and district dollars should not be taken lightly. Cost information can be gathered at the same time that inquiry about program references and presenter availability is made. Again, not all programs or approaches are equally cost-effective. The cost of hiring a well-known expert presenter may include airfare, hotel accommodations, meal cost, and car rental. Cancellation fees (in the event of bad weather or unforeseen emergencies) are also cost issues. Recognized researchers and presenters will be more expensive than their audio- and videotapes will be, and those planning a program should weigh the effectiveness of these alternative approaches.

Teachers within the school should also not be overlooked as potential on-site trainers. There are both fiscal and organizational benefits to be gleaned from this approach in which a school system invests in creating its own on-site trainers. Wu (1987), in reviewing the research on peer trainers, determined that teachers feel more comfortable exchanging ideas, play more active roles in workshops, and receive more practical suggestions when peer trainers conduct workshops. Having on-site trainers has the added advantage of facilitating and extending the cycle of feedback, practice, and coaching. The money a district would have given to an outside expert can be redirected to pay for substitute coverage to allow such coaching.

Time, Place, and Management

Determining the best time, place, and conditions for training is also an important step in planning this model. Good programs can be sabotaged by faulty air-conditioning, broken audiovisual equipment, missing refreshments, and mandatory afterschool sessions. When teachers are tired or uncomfortable, training will fail. With this in mind, attention to the details of physical accommodation should not be left to chance. These details reflect the value those who plan the program place on it and the audience. They send a subliminal message to those attending.

Timing an inservice for effectiveness is never easy. Planners should begin by looking at the big picture, for example, conflicting holidays or events that may cause participants to legitimately excuse themselves in significant numbers. Then consider the actual time of day and length of day to be used. Marathon sessions are rarely effective, and those that come at the end of a long day's work take on marathon dimensions. If an inservice is worth having, it is worth the time required to do it right.

Place is yet another vital factor in planning for a successful inservice. Planners must consider the number who will attend and the activities involved. Auditorium settings will only accommodate large group lectures. Any attempt at small group exercises or discussion will require different suitable facilities. Acoustics and access to effective audio-visual equipment should all be considerations in deciding where an inservice program is held. How effective can the best of presenters be when addressing 100 teachers seated on straight-backed wooden chairs in a cafeteria where neither the air-conditioning nor the public address system works?

The amenities of food and drink also should not be overlooked when planning an inservice. Concern for participants is reflected in attention to these details. Refreshments are necessary icebreakers or intermissions, and to forget them is to doom an inservice to an atmosphere of tedious formality.

Program agendas issued well in advance of an inservice are also a vital part of program management. They are the program plan and can serve to answer questions about details that inevitably arise. They should give participants directions, note starting and closing times, include refreshment and intermission plans, and give presenter biographies. Agendas are a physical reflection of the degree of planning that has gone into a program.

Evaluating Training

Planning for program evaluation is another indispensable step in implementing this model. Planned evaluation should go beyond the traditional closing survey evaluating the presenter's delivery and message. Training is undertaken with the purpose of changing present practice. Therefore, a true measure of training effectiveness is a measurement of change. In determining need, baseline data are gathered. These data, depending on the subject, can come from teacher surveys, classroom observations, disciplinary referrals, teacher and student records of absenteeism, or other concrete evidence of an existing need for change. It follows, then, that training effectiveness can be monitored by reexamining the same data source after training. If training has been effective, there should be positive change, that is, observations showing improvement in instruction, fewer disciplinary referrals, and increased attendance. The particular outcomes one might select to analyze depend on the goals of the improvement effort and the focus of the staff development (Guskey & Sparks, 1991b), but there are concrete ways to monitor effectiveness. If there is no positive change measured in a second look at the data supporting the original need, the training cannot be said to be effective, and it is the responsibility of those who planned the training to then question why. Accountability requires this more rigorous approach to follow-up assessment. It is a waste of time, money, and energy to ignore the need for accountability from program planners as well as participants.

Teacher and Administrator Profiles

Inservice training to change teachers' practice is fairly effective—not with all teachers and not with all teaching practices, but effective enough to change how some teachers do what they do thereby improving achievement, attitudes, and behavior (Gage, 1984). The profile (see Figure 4.2) of the teacher best served by this approach to staff development is that of a teacher who sees a need for change in present repertoire and who is willing to accept the possibility that educational research can provide a way for creating that change. Willingness to change is a key element in making training successful, and this willingness may be either natural or imposed. In the best of all possible scenarios, the teacher wants to change and believes the training offered can lead to the desired change. However, training may also be administratively imposed on teachers found deficient in particular skills. Training, coupled with a performance objectives approach to evaluation, can be an effective tool in the supervision of marginal teachers.

The administrator ideally facilitates planning, implementing, maintaining, and evaluating the inservice and creates ways to monitor accountability for each part of the process (see Figure 4.2). To do this effectively, however, the administrator must believe in the validity of training and its ability to effect change. If either the teacher or

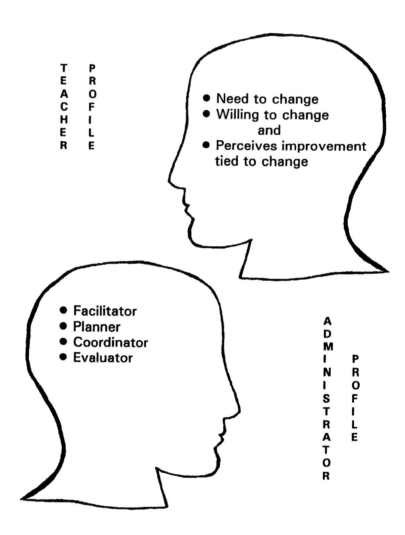

Figure 4.2. Focused-Training Staff Development Model

administrator doubt the value of training, it becomes empty ritual—a gesture of help greeted by superficial response with no commitment on either part. The following discussion questions will help measure the perceived effectiveness of this model.

Discussion Questions

1. Describe the last effective inservice you attended.
2. What made that inservice effective for you?
3. What recent research do you believe would create an effective inservice?
4. Describe training that has changed your performance in the classroom.
5. Describe training that has changed your school's approach to learning.

These questions probe perception of the concept of training by examining the historical perspective participants bring to the experience. Questions 3, 4, and 5 examine perception of research and its application in classroom and school. This model would not prove particularly effective for either a teacher or an administrator who cannot ever recall participating in an effective training session. This model also would not be effective for a teacher or an administrator who has difficulty recalling any recent research of interest. Teachers and administrators who are unfamiliar with the research trends and developments of their profession are unlikely to believe in the effectiveness of such research. These are indications that faith in this model is not there, and inherent skepticism can be a catalyst for failure of this model.

A Planning Guide for Training

Training is never cheap. To the presenter's fee must be added the cost of teacher time, coaching time, and site preparation. In addition, there is the enervating toll exacted by ineffective training or effective training ineffectively supported. These are all factors for which the administrator is ultimately responsible no matter who plans and chooses the program. Figure 4.3 gives an example of a form for use in monitoring the gathering of baseline data, interviewing prospective presenters, determining costs, making selection, and planning for program and follow-up activities. This form is an outline for training program planning and a guide for administrative accountability.

Description of needs assessment process (attach forms used):
Determined training needed:
Description of three programs addressing this need:

Trainer	Phone contact	References	Costs
1.			
2.			
3.			

Trainer selected:
Basis for selection:
Description of training (activities, materials, program format—attachments):
Description of maintenance and coaching activities:

Figure 4.3. Focused-Training Staff Development Planning Guide

Pros and Cons

One obvious positive feature of the training model is its potential cost-effectiveness if done well. Training can be highly cost-effective because of the high participant to trainer ratio (Sparks & Loucks-Horsley, 1990). Training provides large group instruction and feedback during practice sessions. An added plus for this approach is that if the training is indeed effective, as a profession, we do come closer to bridging the gap between research and theory and begin to see the validity of professional sharing. The feedback and coaching aspects of this model can also go a long way in breaking down the walls of isolation that presently envelope most teachers. As they work together in the coaching phase of the model, teachers will share impressions and insights, and they will learn to communicate as professionals discussing their craft. A final point in favor of this model is that if implemented properly from start to finish, it sets clear guidelines for accountability at all levels.

One major drawback to this model, however, rests in the very definition of *training* and all that implies. Adult learning usually consists of two processes: training and education (Rebore, 1991). Training is the process of learning a sequence of programmed behaviors, and education is the process of helping an individual understand and interpret knowledge (S. P. Robbins, 1982). The emphasis in training is on the acquisition of motor skills and on producing simple conditioning methods that improve the ways teachers teach (Rebore, 1991). In contrast, education strives to help teachers dig deeper and analyze the relationship between the variables they encounter in a classroom to understand the complexity of the instructional process. Training is often perceived by teachers as a simplistic answer to the complex problems they face, and so they dismiss it as ineffective without trial. Teachers may also be rebuffed by the idea that as professionals, they are perceived as needing training rather than education.

Another negative aspect of training is that good training frequently follows ineffective training. It is difficult for even good training to stand on its own feet. Ineffective training inservices at any point in a teacher's career will set the stage for rejection. Teachers have been known to say that they have heard it all before, and it just does not work. With this in mind, trainers must strive to overcome historical skepticism by actively assisting teachers to perfect and maintain skills learned. Training should never be simply a single presentation to a large group on a rainy afternoon. Effective training must individualize and extend support well beyond the initial presentation. There really ought to be a warranty of satisfaction with training, considering the time, cost, and effort expended.

A final objection to training that must be overcome is the perception that most training lacks enduring value. Each school year's round of "buzz words" and "current concepts" gives training a faddish air that leaves skeptical teachers whispering to each other that "this too shall pass, and we can only hope soon." Permanent and fundamental change, rather than huge, but temporary, training programs, are needed to ensure that the intellectual and professional life of a teacher becomes more stimulating, demanding, and satisfying (Goldenberg & Gallimore, 1991).

Activities

1. Attend a training staff development program and critique these aspects:
   a. Success in addressing a recognized need
   b. Presenter performance
   c. Training activities
   d. Provision for maintenance and follow-up
   e. Cost versus effectiveness

2. Develop and carry out a needs assessment within your school, department, or subject area; describe the process and results obtained.

3. Research three different approaches to a training topic of your choice, find presenters for each approach, and select a presenter explaining the reasons for your choice.

4. Plan, develop, and implement a staff development program addressing a need in your building and consider these factors:
   a. How will need be assessed?
   b. Why was a particular presenter chosen?
   c. How will effectiveness be assessed?
   d. How will the training be maintained?

5. Develop three different ways to assess the effectiveness of a training program in which you have recently participated.

5

Focused-Research
Staff Development

Although training attempts to bridge the gap between research and practice, the focused-research model for staff development essentially fuses research and practice. This approach to professional growth assumes that practitioners are often the best researchers because they have never left the laboratory. Maehr, Midgley, and Urdan (1992) note that interventions designed by researchers fail because they do not take account of the realities of school and classroom life, and they recommend engaging teachers in the research process to use their expertise and knowledge of practice.

Research itself supports the proposition that classroom teachers can be effective researchers. Real teachers in real classrooms have made significant research findings (Gable & Rogers, 1987; Glickman, 1986; Sparks & Loucks-Horsley, 1990; Sparks & Simon, 1989). In addition, there is an acknowledged need for extensive field testing of theory in educational research. Although many innovations are described as research based, few have been extensively or systematically studied (Guskey & Sparks, 1991b). This is probably due to the difficulty inherent in testing educational theory. The only legitimate laboratory is the classroom, and researchers have no easy access to that laboratory unless they are classroom teachers. As a result, research-based innovation in education usually means that the theory creators referred to some body of research literature when formulating their ideas (Guskey & Sparks, 1991b). In contrast, participation in action research provides a formal way to make teachers' knowledge part of the literature on teaching, bringing them inside the power structure of education (Cochran-Smith & Lytle, 1990) and testing innovation in the classroom.

Focused-action research is a change process encouraging risk taking and raising the status of the educator from skilled technician to scholar practitioner (McKay, 1992). This is the first of a series of professional development models that recognize the importance of providing teachers with an opportunity to grow beyond the classroom while remaining connected to it. Teaching is a field that lends itself to intellectual stagnation and professional frustration because such opportunities are rare. There are relatively few ways in which a teacher is encouraged to have an effect beyond the classroom without leaving it. Educators who tire of the regimen of classroom teaching have really only limited recourse. They become administrators or guidance counselors and leave the classroom permanently. Unfortunately, many of the best do leave the classroom for want of challenge and opportunity to grow. The focused-research model is one of several models in this book that provide an alternative to frustrated flight.

The Method

Focused action research can be conducted by teachers in one of three ways:

1. Individually
2. In collaboration with a university or research group
3. In conjunction with a schoolwide research project (Calhoun, 1993)

In each of these scenarios, the teacher will conduct the research study using a structured approach to scientific inquiry. A typical research cycle would involve the following steps:

1. Identification of the problem
2. Definition of the research question
3. Choice of research method
4. Design of project

Question posed: *something you want to research*
Hypothesis:
Data collection plan:
Data collection analysis:
Conclusions and suggestions for further research: *How do I think this will turn out? Produce a conclusion what do you expect might happen?*

Figure 5.1. Focused-Research Staff Development Planning Guide

5. Collection of data
6. Analysis of data
7. Presentation of results (Oja & Smulyan, 1989)

The project design sheet in Figure 5.1 will assist the teacher researcher in formally deciding how each of these facets of the research project will be handled and in developing a plan for the completion of each step of the study.

Before beginning to design a research project, the teacher researcher should be familiar with existing research on the topic. Project design can then build on those elements of prior research that have proven effective and, from an informed perspective, can modify those elements that have not been effective. Research that merely replicates published research for the purpose of verifying its purported effectiveness also serves a valid scientific purpose if the researcher isolates the factors that invalidate earlier findings. Focused-action research need not discount what has gone before, but it should question the validity of all theory and findings untested in the working classroom.

As teachers enter the field of research, they must also note that there are rules governing research methodology. Teachers conducting action research may need to secure district and parental permission before embarking on some forms of individual research involving students in the classroom setting. Universities engaged in research using human subjects routinely require such permission. Researchers must be ready to explain the purpose of their research design and respond to concerns regarding its implementation.

Although this model's planning and implementation make new and challenging demands on teachers, new and professionally rewarding opportunities are created as well. Successful teacher researchers can publish the results of their studies, add to the existing body of research in education, and help other teachers become more effective without having to leave the classroom themselves.

Teacher and Administrator Profiles

The effect of this research model depends largely on the involvement and support of the administrator, who provides such projects with legitimacy and continuity (Oja & Smulyan, 1989). The administrator must believe in the importance and validity of classroom research as a means of improving the learning process. The administrator must be a risk taker and must encourage risk taking with impunity. The administrator must also provide time and resources needed to take the risks required by action research. This is done by administrative attitude and expectation. Administrators who themselves are risk takers will serve as exemplars and resources to teacher researchers. They will provide teachers with a forum for this creative and challenging approach to professional growth by publishing an in-house research newsletter. They will sponsor research-focused inservices and conferences designed to give teacher researchers an opportunity to share and critique each other's work. Finally, they will recognize and reward teachers who succeed in publishing the results of their work, or in disseminating those results through formalized presentations. Rewards can come in the form of favorable publicity or research stipends, as well as released time to publish and disseminate results.

The profile (see Figure 5.2) of the teacher researcher is that of a patient, meticulous, and inquisitive practitioner. Teachers who like to talk about what they and other teachers specifically do to make a difference in learning are prime candidates for participation in this model's activities. These teachers are ready, willing, and able to try new and different techniques. More important, they are equally ready, willing, and able to declare some techniques successful and others not. These teachers are reflective realists and pragmatists who want results that can be replicated in classrooms other than their own. Teachers who are unafraid to question popular theory and its relationship to practice make good researchers, as do those who are unafraid to say that not every theory works in every classroom but nevertheless want to know why. The following questions are designed to help teachers and administrators assess their own interest and ability to participate in this staff development model.

Self-Assessment

1. Do you know which teaching methods work and why they work?
2. Are you familiar with what the latest research says about effective teaching?
3. Do you ever find yourself disagreeing with popular research theory?
4. Can and do you collect data to test theories and methods?
5. Do you want to make a contribution to education beyond your classroom?
6. Are you a risk taker?
7. Is there value to proving something does not work?

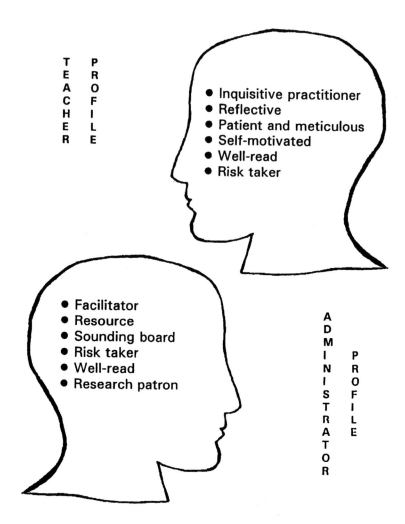

Figure 5.2. Focused-Research Staff Development Model

Pros and Cons

The positive results gleaned from this model when effectively implemented far outweigh any negatives. All teachers *should* be researchers, although not all want to be. The nonroutine nature of teachers' work requires complex, contextual decision making and an inquiry-oriented approach to practice (Lipton, 1993). Improved instruction, more reflective learners, professional growth, and collegial sharing—all can result from involving teachers in classroom research (R. W. Johnson, 1993). Action research is a search for answers to questions relevant to educators' immediate interests, with the primary goal of putting the findings immediately into practice (McKay, 1992).

The downside of this approach to professional growth is that it requires specific skills and a commitment to detail that not all teachers possess. In addition, under the present system, few teachers would have the time to do careful research. Research would be one more demand in an already-overprescribed day.

There is also the question of how teacher-initiated research would fit within the existing educational research hierarchy. Ideally, the product of inquiry and research should be questioned and tested in a refereed forum that does not now exist for classroom teachers. At present, the field of education is socially and intellectually stratified with clear lines of demarcation between those who have left the public school classroom and those who have remained—between university professors, funded researchers, and public school teachers. The field of educational research is presently the domain of those who no longer teach, or never have taught, in regular public school classrooms. Thus, if this model is to be truly effective, it becomes necessary for the profession first to do some internal social engineering. That is, classroom teachers must be welcomed into the realm of educational research and invited to collaborate and test their research hypotheses and conclusions in the classroom *and* in the fire of the refereed journal now exclusively the domain of university and sponsored researchers. Their work as researchers must be accorded collegial respect and scholarly review at all levels of academe. In short, the profession must rid itself of the misguided perception that those who teach can't do viable research. The classroom must become the starting and ending point for all valid research.

Activities

1. Read several articles summarizing research findings regarding the improvement of instruction. Test the findings in your own

instructional setting and write an evaluation of the original study indicating:

a. The validity of the findings

b. Possible reasons for discrepancies

c. Unanswered or related questions requiring further research

2. Develop three questions or hypotheses you feel merit research.

3. Take one question or hypothesis posed in the previous question and examine any research that may have been done on this topic.

4. Develop a research plan for studying the hypotheses you cited in Question 3, using Figure 5.1.

5. Read and evaluate two articles summarizing research in published refereed journals. Critique these articles and the research findings with respect to

a. Clarity of presentation

b. Integrity of the study, that is, composition of study group, factors that might bias study findings, quality control

c. Applicability in the real classroom

6

Merit Pay Staff Development

The merit pay staff development model is in some ways tied to the focused-research model in that it too recognizes the validity of different approaches to the teaching process. A merit pay plan, however, compares and rewards those approaches that prove most successful. This model assumes that some teachers are more capable than others and that introducing a competitive edge to the practice of teaching will lead all teachers to strive to improve performance. It also assumes that the quality of teaching can be objectively measured by its product and that fiscal rewards can thus be objectively and fairly made as an incentive to progress. Merit pay is appropriate where it is clearly observable that one employee is more productive than another and that other employees know or can be told what they must do to receive a merit increase (Keith & Girling, 1991).

In *A Nation at Risk: The Imperative for Educational Reform*, the National Commission on Excellence in Education (1983) recommended that salaries for teaching be increased and be made professionally competitive, market sensitive, and performance based. A similar recommendation was made by the National Science Board Commission on Precollege Education in Mathematics, Science, and Technology (1983) in its *Educating Americans for the 21st Century* report, which called for state and local governments to reward excellence in teaching and provide opportunities for high-quality teachers to move up a salary and status ladder without leaving the classroom. In the wake of these studies, several states have attempted to introduce merit pay into their collective bargaining agreements. Tennessee, for example, instituted a five-level career ladder that links assessed professional competencies and monetary incentives (Keith & Girling, 1991). This approach responds well to the public cry for accountability and to the public perception that teachers live in a nonprofessional cocoon impenetrable to the concerns of parents who must compete for their own dollars in a marketplace economy.

One of the major philosophical objections from teachers to the awarding of merit pay is that the decision to do so is too subjective. Nevertheless, proponents of the concept would contend that every employee's performance can be evaluated in terms of productivity and customer satisfaction. This position is the basis of our free market economy and the progress we have enjoyed as a result of that system. Thus, if some enterprising teachers produce students who perform better than others on objective proficiency tests, why should those teachers not be recognized and rewarded for their success? If some teachers are particularly effective in working with parents to improve student performance and cultivate parental satisfaction, should their success in doing so be left unrecognized and unrewarded? If some teachers have developed ways of helping students with learning disabilities understand, remember, and apply subject matter effectively, is their success and that of their students to be ignored? How can we as a profession hope to improve what we do if, like ostriches, we bury our heads in the mire of pseudo-professionalism and continue to deny that there are some teachers who simply do a much better job than others at helping students at all levels of ability achieve, and who deserve to be recognized and rewarded for their efforts? The field of education should not be the last vestige of a leveling and outmoded Communism that denies and ultimately subjugates initiative and creativity. Merit pay and the competition it would engender are seen as a way to bring the field of education into the marketplace of ideas.

Discussion Questions

1. Do you believe that some teachers are more effective than others?
2. Should this difference be recognized?
3. Should there be an element of competition in the teaching profession?

4. How do other professions acknowledge differences in performance quality?
5. Take a position either favoring or opposing merit pay, and defend that position.

The Method

Thus far, merit pay professional growth plans have taken one of two forms:

1. A plan in which a principal or supervisor assesses individual teachers' performances and decides who deserves to receive merit pay based on that assessment.
2. A plan in which a teacher is awarded merit pay on the basis of documented student performance (Keith & Girling, 1991).

The Dallas School Board has recently approved a pilot test of a new evaluation system that will take students' academic progress into account in rating teachers (A. Bradley, 1995). To make the system fair, district officials have factored in variables that might affect student achievement such as class size, student mobility, socioeconomic levels, language proficiency, and gender. This is an effort to level the playing field before the competition begins.

Stern (1986) introduced the concept of group, unit, or schoolwide merit pay to promote collaboration and dispel some of the objections to merit pay as an incentive to professional growth. In a collective merit pay model, the district proposes to award bonuses to individual schools showing the most improvement. Stern suggests that if merit pay were awarded to the group on the basis of group performance, teachers already performing well would be given the incentive to continue to do so, and they would have leverage to exert peer pressure on those who might not be helping the group effort. Stern's plan may be another, less objectionable, way for schools to inch into a marketplace economy and the competitive incentives to improved performance it promises.

It is, however, also possible for merit pay to be awarded individually by a trained evaluation committee, on the basis of an array of factors, equally weighted, and including

1. *Principal or supervisor assessment of teacher performance.* This assessment should be supported by evidence gathered through the process of clinical supervision.

2. *Student performance.* This should be documented by national, state, and local proficiency tests, grades, awards, and commendations.

3. *Parent assessment of teacher performance.* This should be based on parental perception of communication, homework, assignments, and student progress.

4. *Class makeup.* Teachers who teach students with learning or behavior problems can be evaluated on the degree of individual student improvement and achievement as evidenced by testing.

This method mirrors the approach businesses use in awarding bonuses based on improved production and customer satisfaction. It dispels the argument that teachers with bright, motivated students will always win the competition by making student progress, parental satisfaction, and class makeup factors in determining merit awards.

Ideally, a review board should be charged with evaluating teacher applications for merit pay. This board may include the district superintendent or assistant superintendent, a member of the board of education, the building administrator, and a teacher peer. The review board should receive training to understand testing norms to be used, techniques for evaluating classroom performance, and parent input instruments. Appointment to the board and factors to be considered in making merit awards may be collectively bargained issues. The review board and procedures, to be effective in implementing a merit pay plan, must be perceived as objective and fair.

There is research regarding the degree of merit incentive needed to make a difference in teacher performance. These studies of salary differentials used as motivators indicate that differentials of 20% to 30% are required to have a noticeable effect on motivation (Geis, 1987). At first sight, differentials of this size may seem economically impossible, but differentials of this size are common in the business world, which selectively rewards performance with commissions and bonuses. Also, it must be noted that *not every teacher* will get these differentials under a true merit pay plan. These are not the across-the-board pay increases presently prescribed by negotiated teacher con-

---

The following outline describes the factors that will be used to make merit awards for performance in the position of classroom teacher.

1. Student performance defined by

   - State proficiency test scores

   - School district achievement test scores

   - Quarterly student grades

   - Individual student improvement

   - Student awards and commendations

2. Principal or supervisor assessment of teaching performance by

   - Documented observations

   - Prescribed evaluations

3. Class composition—documented problems and responsibilities

4. Parent assessment by survey and recorded comments

Figure 6.1. Merit Pay Staff Development Planning Guide

tracts. These are merit increases based on individual performance. If indeed schools, as businesses, can be assured of improved productivity through a merit plan, the fiscal outlay will be relatively small compared to the vast amounts of money we now waste on improvement plans and unearned raises that have no effect on a system that remains dysfunctional.

Accountability under this model is inherent in the criteria (see Figure 6.1) established for awarding merit pay. Essentially, a teacher must document satisfaction of the established criteria, and this documentation will be weighed by the committee relative to other applications for merit consideration.

Although quotas or limits to the number of merit awards made may disturb a profession that has historically refused to discriminate between degrees of performance and effectiveness, the fact is that educational funding is limited. If merit awards become watered-down stipends that everybody gets across the board, they will be ineffective—a waste of time for those who truly are exceptional and a waste of money for school boards wishing to foster excellence, not maintain mediocrity.

Teacher and Administrator Profiles

The administrator's role in a merit system is that of a negotiator and gatekeeper, one who must work with the bargaining unit and the board to set the criteria for merit awards and who must then monitor the equity of their implementation in actual practice. The administrator alone should not determine who receives merit pay. An equitable plan should always be based on an array of negotiated criteria to be evaluated by a review board representing those affected. The review board may include the district superintendent or assistant superintendent, a member of the board of education, the building administrator, and a teacher peer. In this way, a range of professionals trained to understand testing norms, classroom performance, and parent input can make an informed group decision to award or deny merit pay. The administrator facilitates the training and functioning of this committee.

As Figure 6.2 indicates, the teacher most likely to succeed in a merit pay plan is one who has proven success in the classroom. This teacher is perceived by colleagues as a capable exemplar. Confident, self-motivated, achieving, and ambitious professionals will find this model an attractive target for their professional energies. This model will give them tangible recognition for a superior effort.

Pros and Cons

On the plus side of the ledger favoring a merit pay staff development plan is the basic belief that a system that rewards initiative will instill initiative. Our present system does not recognize or reward extra effort, and it may therefore actually be thwarting initiative and the progress it engenders. Education does not function as other professions do. Educators do not rely on customer satisfaction as a gradient

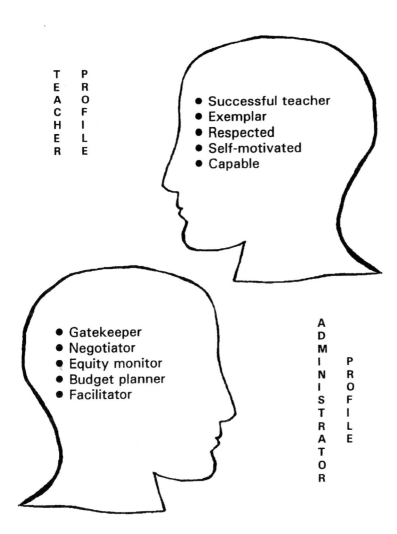

Figure 6.2. Merit Pay Staff Development Model

of their success or professional survival. They serve a virtually captive audience, an audience that is often silently dissatisfied. A plan that gives incentives for improving the way children learn will represent an effort on the part of the profession to allay that dissatisfaction.

There is also something to be said for the example given by having educators join the free market economy, even on this limited scale. We live in a world where competition is the rule not the exception, and students, parents, and community should not perceive teachers as beyond the loop of free market competition. At present, educators are perceived by the public they serve as either unwilling or unable to compete. A merit pay plan for professional growth would help dispel the rampant perception that those who cannot do, teach.

Finally, it must be noted that the innovations we enjoy today were born of competitive urgency. The progress so visible in other fields and professions has been conceived in a competitive forum that rewards initiative and achievement. Educators cannot disavow the effect of competition until they've tried it.

Objections to merit pay plans include the belief held by some that teachers denied merit raises will decrease their efforts. Moreover, some fear that an individualized merit system can interfere with a strong team effort among teachers (Keith & Girling, 1991). Others maintain that merit pay plans discourage teachers who need help from getting it for fear that they will appear weak and unable to compete. Merit pay plans are accused of discouraging communication between teachers and administrators and further isolating teachers from each other thus exacerbating existing serious weaknesses in the public school system (Bacharach, Conley, & Shedd, 1990). Opponents also maintain that there is no fair and objective way to measure production in the classroom. Plans based on student performance are discounted because of the number of interfering factors that affect student scores—the problems of deciding which aspects of the curriculum should be included for testing and how to separate the contribution of one teacher from the next on test scores in view of the cumulative nature of learning (Keith & Girling, 1991).

Proponents of merit pay plans respond that these are simply excuses for inaction and perpetuation of an ineffective status quo that subjugates excellence. They argue that teachers who work harder and achieve observable results should be rewarded (Keith & Girling, 1991). They also argue that merit pay is the fiscal foundation of every other profession. Lawyers who win more cases get more clients and command higher fees. Doctor specialists who earn a reputation for skill and expertise in a given area likewise command fees above those of the general practitioner. They argue that if teaching is ever to join the ranks of recognized professions, teachers, too, must be given the opportunity and incentive to distinguish themselves.

Activities

1. Develop a procedure for awarding merit pay that you feel would be just and equitable. Specifically address the following points:
   a. Who would award merit pay?
   b. What factors would be considered?
   c. What appeal process would be available?
2. In a brief one-page note, summarize your personal feelings regarding the place of merit pay in the teaching profession. This activity is intended to make you clarify and justify your position on this issue. Therefore, you must address these questions:
   a. Do you oppose or favor merit pay?
   b. Why or why not?
   c. How would you respond to opposing arguments?
3. Are there merit pay plans presently in place in public education? Where have they been implemented? How effective are they to date?
4. Explore the philosophical question of why teaching should or should not be a profession responsive to a free market economy.
5. Survey the faculty in your school on the issue of merit pay, and secure their reaction to the following points:
   a. Would they favor a merit pay plan?
   b. Why or why not?

7

School Improvement
Staff Development

In this model, the school's own mission and concerns are used to generate the need to know or the problem to solve. Teachers working on school improvement committees develop plans and programs to achieve the school's mission and address its concerns. In a cooperative learning environment for adults, teachers write curriculum and grants, select texts, evaluate instructional approaches, and plan policies designed to help the school achieve its goals.

The Method

This model assumes that adults learn most effectively when they have a need to know or a problem to solve (Knowles, 1980). Effective schools research shows that such participation in school management by teachers, based on collaborative planning, collegial problem solving, and constant intellectual sharing, can produce student learning gains and increase teacher satisfaction and retention (Darling-Hammond, 1986). The link between staff development and student learning often is not a direct one (Guskey & Sparks, 1991b). Through involvement in school improvement or curriculum development processes, teachers become more appreciative of differing viewpoints and more skilled in group leadership and problem solving (Sparks & Loucks-Horsley, 1990). These changes in perception and skill do ultimately affect student learning and the classroom environment.

Iwanicki (1990) found that the quality of school improvement initiatives is enhanced when the teacher evaluation and school improvement processes are integrated with staff development. Murphy (1987) agrees that one conclusion of the recent school improvement research is that schools work better when plans and activities are coordinated in a common effort to reach important school goals. The basic strategy of this model is to do just that—to develop professional growth opportunities in the context of the school's needs.

Thus teachers and administrators choosing this approach to professional growth must first identify problems to be solved or needs to be addressed within the school. Both mandates and consensus strategies can facilitate success in achieving change through this approach to staff development (Lieberman, 1986; P. Robbins & Wolfe, 1987). For example, recently issued federal and state regulations requiring that special education students be included in regular classrooms serve as an example of how legal mandates can initiate the need for change in the school environment. Administrators, as well as special education and regular education teachers, must understand the new regulations and reassess how they will affect delivery of services to both regular and special education students. Adoption of new district policies, curriculum, or teacher evaluation procedures can similarly mandate change and the corresponding need for professional development responding to that change. In the final analysis, mandates for change will not succeed without grassroots cooperation. Only a mix of top-down and grassroots change efforts can produce effective results (Hirsh & Ponder, 1991). Thus it becomes important to involve a coterie of teachers in the planning and implementation of mandated change. These teachers are essentially empowered to create a plan for seeing that mandated programs are effectively implemented. In contrast, consensus strategies use traditional grassroots needs assessment by the group that will be affected to create a professional development agenda. State, district, and school initiatives can be the focus of needs assessment conducted in any one or combination of the following ways:

1. Surveys and questionnaires
2. Interviews
3. Committee reports
4. Literature reviews

5. Gathering of objective data, for example, test scores, discipline reports
6. Reference to planning documents, for example, 5-year plans
7. State and professional society publications
8. Externally perceived needs (Orlich, 1989)

What is often lacking in these traditional needs assessment strategies, however, is feedback summarizing, reporting, and refining the results of the needs assessment. Teachers are asked to respond individually to an instrument assessing their perception of the school's needs, but individual teachers are seldom given the opportunity to see how colleagues have responded. Instead, a staff development focus is often announced with an air of mystery as to how it was determined. The feeling of consensus is sacrificed to a false sense of efficiency. It is ironic that needs assessment without such feedback inevitably generates optimum inefficiency in that many teachers are alienated by the process itself and never identify with the need designated.

An alternative and more effective approach to consensus planning would be a version of the Delphi technique developed by the RAND Corporation (see focused-training model, Chap. 4) to identify organizational consensus, determine problem areas, and establish priorities by providing detailed feedback and systematic follow-up (Helmer, 1967). In an initial survey, respondents are asked to rank needs as they perceive them. These results are then summarized for the responding group, that is, needs are ranked to reflect group response, and this new list of ranked needs is returned to individual respondents indicating group reaction and asking for another round of ranking needs in light of these results. By repeating this process, needs are narrowed, but individual teachers understand why and feel part of the final decision to narrow and delete.

To implement effective change, by consensus or mandate, teacher groups must

1. Identify needs generated
2. Formulate appropriate responses
3. Develop an action plan
4. Develop procedures to evaluate plan effectiveness

Needs assessment description:	
Identify what is wrong.	

Identified need:
what do we group?

Resources required:

Timelines:	Objectives:
1.	
2.	
3.	

Project evaluation:

Figure 7.1. School Improvement Staff Development Planning Guide

In this approach, teachers write performance objectives as members of school improvement committees, setting timelines for completing the objectives of the group plan and for evaluating the effectiveness of that plan (see Figure 7.1).

However, individual teachers also take responsibility for implementing pieces of the plan. Attention to readiness, planning, training, implementation, and follow-up permeates each effective action plan (F. Wood, 1989), and members of the team or committee share responsibility for the whole and its parts. Plans may deal with the selection of texts, the development of curriculum, school restructuring, the development of a schoolwide discipline plan, or any one of a vast range of issues affecting school environment. Options are the direct product of perceived need determined by legal mandate or a needs assessment process.

Teacher and Administrator Profiles

The profile (see Figure 7.2) of teachers likely to succeed with this model is that of self-disciplined extroverts. They are teachers who enjoy and learn from peer interaction and exchange. Moreover, they are mature and persistent individuals who set objectives and goals and then work steadily to meet them. Teachers who prefer working alone, or who have more immediate and identifiable professional needs, will not benefit from this approach to professional growth, although in some cases such involvement could provide a needed professional or social stretch, as with a teacher new to the profession or school, or a teacher who never participates in the life of the school beyond the classroom door.

The administrator in this model is a resource and coordinator. Particularly in areas where mandates for change are at issue, the administrator will be the primary source of regulatory information to which teachers may not be directly privy. When consensus concerns are at issue, the administrator will coordinate the initial polling and planning. However, once teacher committees are formed, the most effective role for the administrator will be that of an available resource, observer, and sounding board.

Ultimate accountability under this model rests with the teacher committee and its members. It is they who will produce final products or report on the attainment of objectives. Formal procedures for documenting end results, however, help keep the process on track, and individual progress reports keep members accountable.

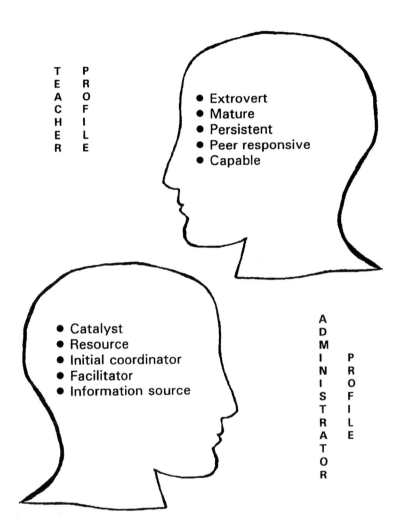

Figure 7.2. School Improvement Staff Development Model

In this model, there are some basic issues of responsibility versus authority that must be addressed if the model is to be implemented successfully. For instance, an administrator must decide if the committee's final recommendations are to be viewed as advisory or binding, and the committee must be aware of how its recommendations will be viewed. Teachers involved in school improvement committees frequently complain that their work was for naught. They spent days and weeks creating plans that are never used. They rewrite curriculum, select texts, and plan program changes that are never funded. From the onset, those who participate in school improvement staff development should be aware of the parameters of their empowerment. The following discussion questions are intended to help administrators and teachers participating in the school improvement model of staff development sort out their feelings concerning these issues.

Discussion Questions

1. Should school improvement committees have ultimate decision-making power?
2. If school improvement committees have ultimate decision-making power, how can they also have responsibility for outcomes of their decisions?
3. As a prospective school administrator, how would you handle public dissatisfaction with a decision you did not actually make?
4. Have you ever served on a school improvement committee that proved ineffective? Why was it ineffective?
5. What could have been done to make the experience worthwhile?

Pros and Cons

This model has a great deal to commend it. It addresses identified needs of the school community and therefore begins with a premise of legitimacy. Neither time nor funding is squandered in this approach. State, district, and school initiatives become the focus of this staff development model, in which individual and institutional goals are meshed. Added pluses are the development of collegial cooperation as well as individual leadership and initiative within the context of the project. Finally, it must be noted that this model, correctly implemented, truly empowers the teachers involved. They literally do participate in the management of the school's and district's programs. This is no small achievement at a time when so much in educational reform is mere lip service to untested empowerment.

The model's negatives are relatively few if it is implemented with proper care. That is, if the participants are teachers genuinely interested in the project posed, with persistent and dedicated dispositions that flourish in group endeavors, this model will do all that we wish for in staff development. However, if the administrator guiding staff development makes inept committee appointments, or fails to support the project once undertaken, this model can become a deadly obstacle to professional growth and school effectiveness. Those who have tasted failure in such efforts are twice as reluctant to give of their time, talents, and enthusiasm in the future. This model derives its strength from productive results achieved in an environment of collegial respect, sharing, and caring. It is not the right model for every teacher, nor is it the right model for every school administrator. Only those administrators who truly know and trust the judgment of the teachers in their buildings, have the respect of those teachers, and are willing to commit resources available to building needs should view this model as a viable option for professional growth. Administrators must be ready, willing, and able to share power under this model. Ultimately, they relinquish the right to make management decisions on some issues to the school improvement committee. This requires a degree of trust that some administrators simply cannot muster and that a school board may not condone. All these factors play a role in the unspoken pros and cons of the school improvement staff development model.

Activities

1. Describe any school improvement projects your school has undertaken in the past 5 years. Assess their effectiveness and the contributing factors.
2. What school improvement projects do you wish your school would undertake?
3. Provide data to justify the concerns you have expressed in Activity 2.

4. Describe your participation in a school improvement project:
   a. How were you chosen to participate?
   b. What was the goal of the project?
   c. How many teachers participated in this project?
   d. What was the final product of this project?
   e. Was this project effective?
   f. Why or why not?

5. Analyze your feelings as a member of a school improvement committee. Specifically, discuss what you found most and least rewarding about the process.

6. Discuss your position concerning the authority of the school improvement committee:
   a. Should the committee's recommendations be unilaterally implemented?
   b. Why or why not?

7. How can any conflict between authority and responsibility be resolved? Do you believe that teachers should have a role in school management, and if so, should this role have any limitations?

8

Internal Career Ladder Staff Development

The internal career ladder model, like the focused-research and school improvement models, gives teachers the opportunity for growth beyond their assigned classrooms. The internal career ladder, however, severs the classroom tie to professional development in whole or in part. Career ladders, under this model, reward teachers for taking on responsibilities within the school beyond those in their regular classrooms. Career ladders offer opportunities for promotion and greater compensation to members of a profession that until recently was considered a dead-end occupation (Parker, 1985). This model of staff development assumes that there are some teachers who need to do more than teach, who need to leave the classroom for a time, in whole or in part, to grow professionally and then return to the classroom rejuvenated, fulfilled, and committed. Without the career ladder option, teacher professional growth is virtually tied to the classroom, a prospect that indeed leads some good, but temporarily bored and frustrated, teachers to abandon the classroom totally. These bright, but unchallenged, professionals become administrators, counselors, or consultants in their search for more creative outlets and release from the routine of classroom teaching, or they leave education entirely. The career ladders described provide a professional alternative for curbing this enervating exodus.

The Method

Teachers involved in internal career ladder programs have an unlimited range of professional growth options if school districts would only capitalize on their potential. They can mentor other teachers, coordinate academic and public relations programs, write curriculum, write and administer grants, participate in peer coaching, manage discipline, serve as administrative interns, and manage the endless array of worthy internal tasks that now go undone in most school districts. Ideally, career ladder options should be developed and posted as job openings would be (see Figure 8.1), with job descriptions citing specific qualifications and job responsibilities. Candidates should be interviewed by a school governance panel required to render its decision regarding appointment based on the candidate's qualifications, experience, and vision with respect to the job's demands.

Accountability for performance under this model should be tied to job descriptions. In other words, when career ladder assignments are created they should list specific performance expectations, and these should be used to evaluate performance periodically throughout the term of appointment. A sample career ladder job description and evaluation form appears in Figure 8.1. Teachers engaged in career ladder activities may also develop professional portfolios citing their accomplishments, and these can be used in supervising and assessing career ladder performance. Because the equitable distribution of intrinsic and extrinsic rewards is an integral part of the career ladder model, performance must be supervised and assessed as part of the professional growth process.

The incentives and rewards earned by teachers assuming added responsibilities may include

1. Differentiated roles with additional job privileges as well as responsibilities
2. Opportunities for greater expression and professional autonomy
3. Extrinsic rewards such as pay, praise, and promotion (Parker, 1985)

Although career ladders may exist with or without financial incentives, research shows that by a four to one margin, the general public

Position title:	
Position qualifications::	
Position responsibilities:	
Performance evaluator: Position:	
Date:	Performance evaluation (attach specifics):
1.	
2.	
3.	
Summative assessment and recommendations:	

Figure 8.1. Internal Career Ladder Staff Development Planning Guide

and teachers themselves favor development of career ladder plans with extra pay for extra duties (Parker, 1985). D. Katz and Kahn (1978) report that extrinsic rewards and incentives improve performance in many occupations: "Pay for performance leads to an increase in performance." Thus career ladders with extrinsic rewards are ideal. However, in the present educational climate, money is not always available, and the value of the alternative intrinsic incentives of title, power, and privilege should not be underestimated. In fact, intrinsic rewards may actually give rise to extrinsic rewards in the event that teachers functioning successfully within unpaid career ladders create permanent rungs for themselves by assuming responsibility for programs a district comes to find indispensable. It should also be recognized that administrative training and the validation of expertise in teaching, curriculum writing, grantwriting, or sundry other career ladder functions give the career ladder participant background and experience that may, at some future point in time, translate into dollar-and-cents recognition in or out of the school environment.

As with each of the models presented, the internal career ladder presents several unique philosophical and implementation issues for discussion.

Discussion Questions

1. If teachers serving in career ladder positions are taken out of the classroom, who will replace them, and how should these replacement positions be defined?
2. What length of time should be assigned to career ladder appointments, and how should this be determined?
3. Should career ladder positions be part of the negotiated collective bargaining agreement? Why or why not?
4. Who should evaluate career ladder position effectiveness?

Teacher and Administrator Profiles

The profile (see Figure 8.2) of the teacher best suited for participation in the career ladder is that of an independent teacher leader and risk taker. These teachers share one or more of the following distinctive behaviors as they function within the school environment:

1. *They challenge the process.* They are risk takers who capitalize on opportunities and are willing to try new things.
2. *They are articulate and inspire a shared vision.* They like teamwork and instinctively nurture the talent and energy of others.
3. *They enable others to act.* They create the conditions for themselves and others to achieve goals set.
4. *They model the way.* By example, they inspire those around them to follow suit (Kouzes & Posner, 1990).

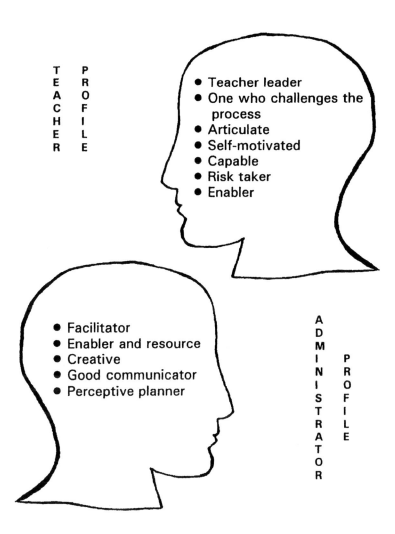

Figure 8.2. Internal Career Ladder Staff Development Model

Some or all of these qualities are needed to inspire individual and group commitment to the career ladder leader because these teachers will take on new roles of authority outside of the classroom and responsibility for the performance of other adults. To do this effectively, they must engender collegial respect and confidence.

The administrator in the career ladder scenario is a creative enabler. Administrators know firsthand what needs to be done to make their schools function more effectively. They also have a unique opportunity and responsibility to discover and nurture the untapped skills and interests of teachers within their buildings. Thus administrators using this model match teacher skills to building needs, create new roles for teachers—that is, rungs on the career ladder—and provide incentives wherever possible. Enabling also involves anticipating and removing obstacles to the success of the career ladder option, such as the perception of favoritism, and union opposition to appointments beyond the contract's reach. To effectively implement a career ladder, administrators must have the trust and respect of faculty, union, and board of education.

Pros and Cons

One obvious positive feature of the internal career ladder posed in this model is that it serves the professional needs of the school and district while giving educators a professional growth option long enjoyed by other professions. Teachers can at last have professional growth experiences outside of the classroom without permanently leaving the classroom. They can take on the new empowered roles promised in the restructuring movement as part of personal professional growth plans and be either intrinsically or extrinsically rewarded for their efforts.

Another controversial, but positive, aspect of this model is that it, like merit pay, will introduce a competitive edge to the profession of teaching for those who wish to compete. This model, like the merit pay model, recognizes that teachers are not all the same. They differ from each other in their professional needs as well as their professional capabilities. Not every teacher will want to climb the internal career ladder. Not every teacher will be able to climb the career ladder. Teachers who are capable and interested will compete for positions beyond classroom responsibilities, and choices will have to be made. But in an economy that draws its lifeblood from marketplace demand and competition, one cannot help but again wonder if this competitive edge might not lend new vigor to the way schools function. Where career ladders are in place, teachers find them a welcome outlet for stifled ambition.

It is this philosophical debate over the role of competition in education, however, that is central to the arguments against the internal career ladder model for professional development, arguments similar to those opposing merit pay. Opponents argue that teachers denied extrinsic incentives will grieve and appeal if they feel denials are arbitrary and capricious (Parker, 1985). Thus the challenge for implementing such a program will be to create a selection process with no hint of being arbitrary and capricious, a task opponents deem impossible.

Opponents also object to the inherent limits posed by career ladders. Specifying that particular duties and responsibilities belong to teachers at particular levels of the system virtually guarantees there will be quotas on the number of positions at each level of the career ladder, and opponents maintain that quotas undermine the claim that career ladders are professional growth opportunities open to all teachers solely on the basis of individual qualifications (Bacharach et al., 1990).

Another opposing argument focuses on a resultant threat to collegiality. Opponents maintain that the very capabilities that distinguish teacher leaders from others—risk taking, collaboration, role modeling—produce tensions between them and colleagues (Wilson, 1993). In short, there are those who see the differentiated assignments and incentives of this model as fruit from the forbidden tree destined to destroy professional commitment to teaching. Duckett (1984), for example, has suggested that dollars and status can become more important than performing job tasks; that is, the goal of improved teaching would be displaced by the goal of increased pay or status.

Proponents of career ladders would respond that the present system, which claims to preserve collegiality by renouncing competition and leveling fiscal rewards, is not working. As school quality and job satisfaction plummet, there is an obvious need to change the existing system. Other professions that have welcomed competition, differentiated professional roles, and encouraged incentives for increased responsibility have made significant progress. Education has not. Perhaps it is time to examine the notion that teaching may improve in a competitive professional forum. This is what other professions routinely do in an effort to renew themselves and their programs. Doctors and lawyers are free to research, to write, to take on new and different challenges within their fields while maintaining or limiting their actual practices. As long as the opportunity to participate is equitable and fair, why should teachers not be given the same options? There is a great deal to be done in improving education in and out of the classroom at all levels, and much of it can best be done by capable practitioners who know the educational environment. Schools have routinely ignored the expertise within their walls and opted for uninformed external expertise rather than informed diversification within their ranks.

Activities

1. Analyze your own building needs and develop a list of five career ladder functions.
2. Interview your building principal concerning feasible career ladder opportunities.
3. Interview your building principal concerning perceived obstacles to implementing an internal career ladder at the building level. Discuss ways in which these obstacles may be overcome.
4. Research the ways in which other schools have succeeded in implementing successful career ladder programs.
5. Develop a job description for a career ladder position within your building including the following factors:
   a. Description of qualifications
   b. Description of responsibilities
   c. Description of selection procedure
   d. Description of supervision and evaluation process
   e. Discussion of reward structure
6. Interview a teacher who has participated in a career ladder program concerning
   a. Program perceptions
   b. Rewards of participation
   c. Drawbacks of participation
7. Research and report on the types of reward structures used to implement existing career ladder programs.

9

External Career Ladder Staff Development

The external career ladder is a new and relatively untested model for professional growth. It, like the internal career ladder, gives teachers opportunities for professional growth outside the classroom. It, like the internal career ladder, allows the teacher to leave the classroom temporarily or permanently to pursue other avenues of educational challenge. However, the external career ladder gives teachers opportunities for professional growth beyond classroom, school, and district. Although there have been some attempts to afford teachers such opportunities—through full or minisabbaticals, for example—this model suggests more formal, frequent, and less expensive approaches for having teachers actively participate in professional opportunities in the world beyond their immediate schools and districts that will have an effect on education.

The Method

Perhaps the best way to explain how this model works is to discuss some possible plans for implementing it. One such plan would be a university exchange program in which skilled classroom practitioners were invited to teach for a semester in university teacher preparation programs while university professors in these same programs take over public school classrooms in an effort to keep abreast of the changing reality of the public school classroom. Participation in such an exchange could be a learning experience for participants at each level and will give them new insights and credibility in each other's eyes. Professors in colleges of education are often accused of teaching from yellowed notes about students and classrooms they left long ago, and classroom teachers are often perceived by academia as the reason children seem to be learning less these days. Their lack of enthusiasm, dedication, patience, and pedagogy are blamed for the failure of research to inform practice. Role exchanges can help each see the other's side of the picture up close and personal, and this dose of reality can provide a stimulating forum for discussion during and after the experience.

University exchanges can also be advantageous in the area of undergraduate counseling. Public school counselors would bring a unique perspective to the task of counseling college freshmen. They would also gain new insights into the challenges facing college students that would better inform their counseling efforts when they return to the public school.

Another version of the external career ladder could involve an exchange of teachers at different schools and levels in the district, or with teachers in other districts that have exemplary programs. Articulation among schools and teachers inside and outside of a district is a vital untapped resource. We have much to learn from each other, and exchanges can facilitate this learning process with relatively little expense and difficulty. For example, at a time when policies of inclusion are being mandated in special education, it would be beneficial for a school contemplating this change to have one of its teachers participate firsthand in a program of inclusion that appears to be succeeding. It would also be beneficial for a teacher who has worked in such a program to spend time as a visiting expert in a school contemplating adoption of a similar plan.

Other possible exchanges could be made with educational consultants, program coordinators, or central office personnel. Educators in these roles have a need to work in classrooms firsthand to have a realistic perspective of how decisions they make as administrators will affect what happens in classrooms. By the same token, classroom teachers will benefit from the chance to see the big picture in which administrative planning takes place. Exchanges such as these could be particularly beneficial to teachers seeking administrative certification or engaged in graduate work and research in curriculum, administration, or subject area supervision. At present, certificates and degrees are awarded for completing programs emphasizing class-room study rather than field-based experience. The need for field experience at all levels of certification, not just the initial preparation of teachers, is evident, but there remain few plans for providing substantive field experiences. Thus the image of untested expertise persists, widening the gap between research and practice, and be-tween administrator and teacher. These role exchanges could dispel that image by providing participants with new understandings of what each role entails.

In some areas, exchanges with businesses and industries could be beneficial. For example, business, industrial arts, and computer sci-ence teachers could profit from seeing how the businesses they pre-pare their students to enter really function. By spending a sustained period in the work world, they themselves have a better under-standing of what students need to succeed. Many businesses already see such exchanges as opportunities for them to have a hand in the preparation of future employees and to contribute to a worthwhile community endeavor.

Product development and marketing is yet another external career ladder approach. As noted in an earlier discussion, there are many teachers doing great things in their classrooms. They have personally developed unique and successful approaches to teaching. They write and revise curriculum to address changing issues and needs. They create programs and tests and texts. They create and teach in so many ways, but that creativity and teaching has been limited by district geography and the time constraints of traditional classroom assign-ments. In business and industry, when an employee makes a discov-ery, finds a better way of doing things, business quickly moves to assist in the development, dissemination, and marketing of a formal-ized product. It is time that school districts did the same, that is, assist teachers in publishing and promoting their creative and successful ideas and products. If, for example, a teacher is a particularly gifted inservice presenter, the school district should assist the teacher in developing and marketing this service. Teachers engaged in staff development presentations may also produce audiotapes, video-tapes, or printed materials to supplement their presentations. In a similar manner, schools can facilitate teachers' writing texts, publish-ing research, and serving as project consultants. These accomplish-ments, as the other examples, reach beyond the employing school district but can bring esteem, satisfaction, and possible profit sharing to teacher and district. This approach has the added advantage of stimulating research and development within the field. A person's greatest opportunity for growth is systematic inquiry into one's own learning, and classrooms are where experimentation for the sake of improvement must take place (Hirsh & Ponder, 1991). Why should schools not follow the example of teaching hospitals and become centers for the research, development, and dissemination of learning?

Accountability in this model can be measured in terms of completion of performance objectives mutually predetermined by the administrator and teacher. As Figure 9.1 indicates, these objectives and the conditions for attaining them should be formalized in advance.

In essence, a performance contract should be developed specifying objectives, qualifications, responsibilities, and mode for evaluating final outcomes of an external placement. The exchanges, for example, can yield results such as published reports or formal presentations on the experience. One such exchange report was shared in the article "Quantum Leap—A Teacher and a Consultant Exchange Jobs" (Lier & Bufe, 1993), in the October 1993 issue of *Educational Leadership* dealing with the theme "new roles, new relationships."

This is a new and different approach to professional growth—one most teachers may never have dared contemplate. It is also an approach that some, perhaps many, teachers would find burdensome and unduly threatening. The prospect of being required to function successfully in a strange environment and an unfamiliar role does have its challenges. However, before the concept is rejected out of hand, let us take a moment to discuss and compare our individual reactions to the external career ladder model.

Discussion Questions

1. Have you ever wanted to work outside of your school or district? Why or why not?
2. Describe an external career ladder opportunity you would find personally fulfilling.
3. Use Figure 9.1 to plan for this external career ladder opportunity.
4. What concerns do you personally have about participating in this model?
5. How would you feel about others participating in this model?

Position title:		
Position qualifications::		
Position responsibilities:		Position Objectives:
Location:	Supervisor:	Position:
Observation date:	Observation commentary (specific discussion attached):	
1.		
2.		
3.		
Summary assessment and recommendations:		

Figure 9.1. External Career Ladder Staff Development Planning Guide

Teacher and Administrator Profiles

The teacher most likely to benefit from participation in an external career ladder is a mature, intelligent, and confident self-starter. This teacher's profile (see Figure 9.2) is marked by tested experience and success in the classroom and an innate desire to challenge the status quo. This individual must be self-disciplined and capable of dealing with the exigencies of functioning in an unfamiliar environment. Communication and public relations skills are also integral to success in this model because the external career ladder model involves outside collaboration for each approach to be successful. The list of traits for success with this model is more extensive than that for any of the other models because the relationships forged are more complex and unpredictable. Not all teachers are capable of adapting to this avenue of staff development, and many would not want to try. This model is the embodiment of risk taking because it places the teacher in roles beyond classroom and district with the mission to produce and achieve for personal and professional profit.

The administrator who facilitates implementation of this model must also be a risk taker and an effective communicator. This is untested ground for a profession that has dug its heels into traditional turf. Administrators who dare to forge ahead must be true leaders with charisma, foresight, and persistence. This model demands a willingness to beg, plead, cajole, barter, negotiate, and rationalize with participants and observers inside and outside of the school environment. It also demands creativity, the ability to find a way to accomplish what others will profess to be impossible: making teaching a profession with many new options for professional growth beyond the immediate classroom that reflect those found in the business world.

Pros and Cons

The primary advantage to this approach is that it provides an avenue of growth for the gifted and self-starting veteran teacher. These teachers have much to give the profession, and they have the maturity and self-discipline to make that contribution with minimal administrative supervision. What they need instead is the administrative support, understanding, and ingenuity to help them reach their full professional potential. Presently, these same gifted, but bored, individuals can undermine staff development they personally perceive a waste of time and effort. They are the voices from the center of the auditorium quietly declaring, "We've already tried that, and it didn't work," or "So what else isn't new?" They are respected by their colleagues for their professional expertise, experience, and inde-

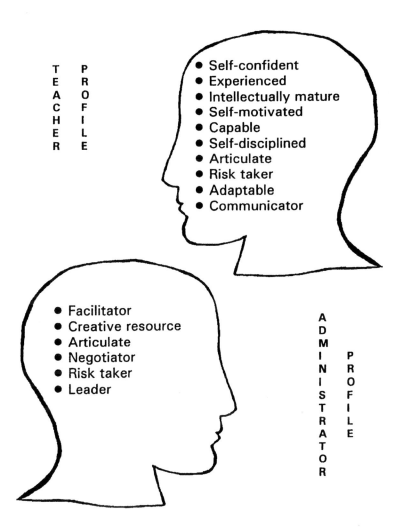

Figure 9.2. External Career Ladder Staff Development Model

pendence, and so those disgruntled whispers don't go unnoticed. If professional development planners continue to ignore their needs, they will continue to communicate their own professional disillusionment to the next generation of teachers, sabotaging any real prospect for meaningful change.

This model also has the advantage of putting teachers where the action is and allowing them to take firsthand responsibility for global change. They become change agents. Depending on the project chosen, teachers can be involved in training new teachers, helping school districts other than their own implement new programs, writing textbooks and computer programs, or serving as liaisons between the school and business communities. Under this model, they are not simply trained; they become the trainers. They are not evaluated; they are the evaluators. They are not passive recipients; they are active creators and implementors of theory and practice valued in a forum other than their home base.

The downside of this model is that it takes time to deal with the details of implementing such a plan for one or more teachers. There will be obvious questions about contractual issues and details such as salary, benefits, and site supervision that must be addressed in arranging such experiences. The important thing to remember, however, is that difficult does not mean impossible. It merely means that creative negotiations must be pursued. In many ways this model is just requiring administrators, school districts, and collective bargaining agents to do for teachers what the research and literature require teachers to do for students—individualize for optimum achievement. We all have an inherent dislike for having our individuality ignored, and when it is ignored creativity is sacrificed to mediocrity.

Activities

1. Describe one possible external career ladder option you feel would be feasible in your own district.
2. Interview an external agency or employer you believe might participate in an external career ladder program concerning the following factors:
   a. Support of the concept
   b. Possible career ladder opportunities
   c. Qualifications for participation
   d. Description of responsibilities
   e. Program advantages and obstacles

3. Interview a teacher who has taken leave from teaching responsibilities to participate in an external career ladder activity
   concerning
   a. Perception of the experience
   b. Rewards and drawbacks
   c. Value of program to professional development
4. In a group, brainstorm five possible external career ladder
   opportunities.
5. Develop a job description for one of the external career ladder
   opportunities presented in the previous question, noting
   a. Qualifications
   b. Responsibilities
   c. Objectives
   d. Selection process

10

Self-Directed Staff Development

This last model strikes at the heart of the philosophical issues surrounding the ultimate personalization of professional development. That is, it brings into question who will finally decide the course of professional growth to be pursued. Although each of the models discussed thus far is different, the process of choosing a model has been a joint teacher-administrative effort, in most cases, with the option of an administrative mandate where appropriate. In the self-directed staff development model, the teacher alone sets the focus, determining the personal learning goals and selecting activities that will result in achievement of these goals (Sparks & Loucks-Horsley, 1990). Malcolm Knowles (1984, 1986) maintained that adult learners have a great degree of self-directedness, have experiences that form a knowledge base, and learn by solving problems. In keeping with Knowles's premise, this model assumes individuals can best judge their own learning needs and that they will be most motivated when they select their own learning goals based on their personal assessment of their needs (Sparks & Loucks-Horsley, 1990). This self-directed, teacher-concern approach involves skills such as decision making and strategy planning, and the processes of negotiation and evaluation (Tracy & MacNaughton, 1993), but these skills rest primarily with the teacher.

Knowles's theory is supported by considerable research on adult learning. As early as 1978, Boyan and Copeland recognized that needed change in behavior must come from within a teacher, not be imposed from outside. Rogers (1969) believed that the only learning that significantly influenced behavior was self-discovered, self-appropriated learning. Glickman (1990), however, recognized that psychological, cognitive, and developmental variables have an effect on a teacher's degree of self-direction. In addition, Levine (1989) found that individuals differing in stages of development have differing personal and professional needs. Teachers, like their students, differ in the very ways in which they assimilate knowledge and adopt new skills as well. All individuals differ in the ways they perceive and process information and in the modes of learning that are most effective for them (Dunn & Dunn, 1978). Thus one can conclude that programs in which individuals select both the form and substance of learning are a valid approach to professional development.

The Method

In the self-directed model, teachers are not limited to choosing projects directly related to classroom or professional performance. They may become involved in enrichment or supplemental activities that have only a tangential effect on immediate classroom performance. They may engage in educational research and writing, or some aspect of study not immediately germane to their teaching or professional assignment. This model precludes administrative interference with project selection. Instead, it assumes that teachers who are challenged and fulfilled in any chosen forum will be better teachers as a result of that challenge and fulfillment. A history teacher who chooses to attend law school, a math teacher engaged in the study of French, or a language teacher who embarks on a quarter of travel would all be effectively using this model for professional growth.

A form such as that in Figure 10.1 can be used to assist the teacher in planning the project. Note that there must be a goal delineated in behavioral terms. A year off for rest and recuperation is not one of this model's options. Time and resources needed are noted, as well as the anticipated outcomes and effects the project will have on the teacher's professional development, on the teacher's performance in the classroom, and on school, district, and professional community.

[Handwritten margin note top: "not administratively controlled — anything that benefits the tcher."]

Goal (state in behavioral terms): *[handwritten: can do outside of Day / what will make you more fulfil]*	
Objectives with timelines: *[handwritten: I will do ___ term]*	
Dates:	Objectives to be completed:
1. *[handwritten: not exactly]*	
2.	
3.	
Resources needed to complete objectives: *[handwritten: need time & money]*	
Anticipated outcomes:	
For students *[handwritten: informed about ___]*	
For school and district *[handwritten: provide programs / helps c curriculum]*	
For profession *[handwritten: better tcher / publish]*	

[Margin handwritten: "Be specific"; "What makes you a more professional"]

Figure 10.1. Self-Directed Staff Development Planning Guide

In this model, it remains the teacher's prerogative to determine the degree of administrative involvement beyond this planning statement. In the end, it will also be the teacher who determines the degree of success attained in reaching the objectives and goals the teacher has set. Professional introspection is this model's keystone.

Travel, university study in a new area, and participation in interesting, but not directly related, professional enrichment programs are only a few of the potential avenues for self-directed development. Sabbaticals, release time, and grant support are just a few of the ways in which teachers can be supported in these efforts. Publicly acknowledging the accomplishments of these innovative educators, disseminating the results of their work, and incorporating their experiences into the school's program are other ways that school administrations can support teachers who choose this model for professional growth.

Philosophically, this model represents a true break with traditional professional development practice. In doing so, this approach raises questions of accountability and issues of ultimate control not posed by the other models presented. The following discussion questions explore some of these issues and the attitudes that must be overcome to make this model feasible. They also set the stage for creating an array of options that can be used in implementing the model.

Discussion Questions

1. What limits, if any, should be placed on a teacher's self-directed plan for professional growth? Give a rationale for such limitations.
2. Brainstorm nontraditional personalized professional growth plans. What have you always wanted to do to maximize your professional growth in a nontraditional way?
3. How could you justify your plan to your district administration?

Teacher and Administrator Profiles

The profile (see Figure 10.2) of the teacher best served by this model is once again that of an intellectually mature, reflective, perceptive, and self-motivated individual, a teacher with no immediate and visible instructional problems. Reliance on self-assessment and analysis

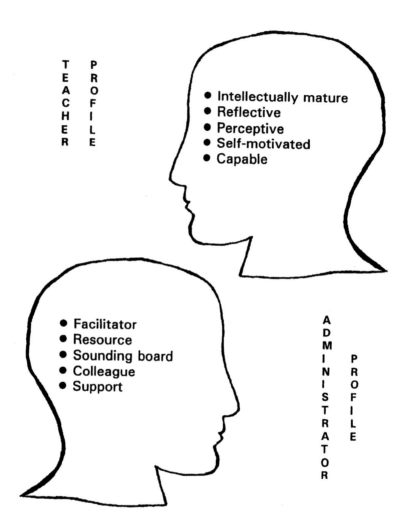

Figure 10.2. Self-Directed Staff Development Model

is a key characteristic of self-directed professional development (Loucks-Horsley et al., 1987). Teachers with identified problems in the classroom, and who need administrative assistance and direction in addressing these problems, would not qualify for this avenue of professional development.

Essentially, teachers using this model must be capable of assessing their own needs and planning ways to address these needs. Human beings' potential for self-guided growth is limited by their cognitive structures, past experiences, and repertoires of skills (Knox, 1977). Thus teachers new to the profession are also unlikely to have the cognitive experiences and maturity to benefit from this approach. Therefore, all these factors must be weighed in determining if a teacher is ready for self-directed professional development, and participation should be based on a review of the teacher's record of achievement in and out of the classroom.

Implementation of this model casts the administrator primarily in the role of a gatekeeper. Although the administrator cannot influence or control project selection, the administrator can decide who may participate in this avenue of professional development based on existing performance records. To do otherwise would be a breach of the administrator's duty to the district. It would be irresponsible to allow teachers who need help in becoming good teachers to ignore their immediate professional responsibilities. It would also be administratively irresponsible to reward or burden professionally immature teachers with this degree of self-determination. The administrator must exercise informed judgment in deciding who may elect this model of professional development.

Once selection is made, however, the administrator assumes the role of a potential resource, an available sounding board, and a project facilitator providing the time, the materials, and the moral support the teacher may request. Initial support of this process takes place when the administrator helps the teacher formalize professional growth objectives for this model and systematically plan for their achievement.

Pros and Cons

As with each of the models presented, there are philosophical, economic, and implementation pros and cons. In the case of the self-directed professional development model, there are obvious objections to giving the teacher exclusive control of the professional improvement process. How can a school district be certain that the teacher's goals and objectives will ultimately benefit students in the district? How can a district relinquish the authority to monitor and approve the direct and indirect use of school funds for professional development? If teachers become involved in projects not germane to their classroom assignments, will their work suffer?

Control plays a significant role in how we presently run schools, and this model requires that boards of education and administrators relinquish control for the sake of true professional development. It requires that teachers be accorded the faith and respect given other professionals to make professional growth choices that may not appear immediately relevant to anyone but themselves. In the final analysis, defense of this model rests on the premise that schools will be better places to learn only when professionally mature and dedicated teachers make them so. Teachers who are intelligent and motivated professionals are needed, and professional self-determination, the keystone of motivated intelligence, may be the missing piece in the puzzle of school improvement.

The centrally controlled and monitored approach to professional development most schools presently use does not work for everyone. To the extent that it does not, school districts are wasting time and money both directly and indirectly. There is a direct loss in that the programs, for all their central control, have not produced the tangible improvement sought. There is also an indirect loss of untapped human capital, in that we have yet to know what might have been had true professionalism been nurtured. In short, we must ask what degree of creativity and professionalism has been sacrificed to administrative control.

This is not to say that accountability for public funding can be ignored. It cannot. Today, accountability demands require that influence on student outcomes be a principal focus in evaluating staff development programs (Guskey & Sparks, 1991a). If a school district's professional development budget is to fund teacher improvement projects, there must be some way to be sure that projects will ultimately benefit school and student interests. The traditional way to do this would be to require teachers to file a culminating report indicating exactly how they have used their professional development experience in the interest of students. More creative alternatives ensuring accountability might include teachers' giving seminars on research or study undertaken, producing curriculum, writing books, teaching new skills learned—in essence, producing a professional development product designed to share with the professional community. In the end, however, we must remember that happy, productive staff members cannot but benefit students (Raebeck, 1994).

Those who would oppose this model's use could take issue with the control exercised by the administrator in determining who may elect to participate in self-directed staff development. If indeed this is the pivotal model for professional growth, why should there be barriers to any teacher's participation? How can the professionally immature be expected to grow if they too are not given the opportunity to self-direct? If failure is indeed an aspect of learning, is there not value even in self-directed professional plans that go awry?

Activities

1. Discuss the self-directed staff development model with three colleagues and summarize their responses to this approach.
2. Describe self-directed staff development activities you could undertake in each of the following areas:
   a. Professional growth (degree and certification programs, publications, leadership roles, etc.)
   b. Organizational growth (committee membership, program development, service activities, etc.)
   c. Personal growth (travel, study, new experiences, etc.)
3. Discuss your perception of the major drawbacks to this approach to professional development.
4. Interview a professional who is not an educator (doctor, lawyer, business executive), concerning ways in which that person plans for professional growth.
5. Review and discuss mandated continuing education requirements for educators in your state. How do they relate to this model's goal?
6. Where do you see yourself professionally 5 years from now?
7. Develop a professional growth plan for each of the next 2 years that will bring you closer to achieving the professional goal you set for yourself in Question 6.
   Year 1 objective:
   Year 2 objective:

11

A Combined Approach to
Staff Development

In the best of all professional development worlds, teachers should
have the opportunity to create individualized professional development plans that may incorporate one or more of the models discussed in this book. For example, a skilled veteran teacher should be
able to participate in a merit pay program while working on a the-
matic school improvement project. A novice teacher might engage in
the classroom-centered staff development with a peer coaching component, and at the same time receive focused training in cooperative
learning. A midcareer teacher having second thoughts about teaching
as a profession could be counseled to participate in a self-directed
staff development program with either an internal or an external
career ladder component. Teacher writers and researchers might
choose the option of continuing classroom teaching while doing
focused research designed for publication and dissemination through
participation in an external career ladder arrangement. These combinations of staff development models, if developed solely by the
teacher, are the very essence of self-directed professional growth.

The Method

Method, teacher profile, administrative profile, and accountability requirements will vary with the models combined. Combining
strategies for professional development recognizes not only a

teacher's individuality but also a teacher's motivational complexity. Teachers are not one dimensional. Riegle (1987) created a conceptual framework for planning teacher professional development that identifies five general areas in which professional growth may occur:

1. *Instructional development*, emphasizing the development of skills involving instructional technology, microteaching, media, courses, and curricula

2. *Professional development*, emphasizing growth of individual faculty in their professional roles

3. *Organizational development*, emphasizing the needs, priorities, and organization of the institution

4. *Career development*, emphasizing preparation for career advancement

5. *Personal development*, emphasizing life planning, interpersonal skills, and the growth of faculty as individuals

Classroom-centered and focused-training staff development plans address the teacher's need for instructional development. Self-directed, focused-research, and merit pay plans deal with professional development in that they each give the teacher the opportunity to grow as a professional without leaving the classroom. Organizational improvement and focused research can address organizational development as they work on themes and research topics vital to school improvement efforts. The internal and external career ladders together with self-directed planning focus on the career advancement and life-planning concerns of career and personal development.

Pros and Cons

As with the other models discussed, there are gains and losses inherent in combining one or more staff development models. The primary positive of this type of plan is that it humanizes the process of professional development, recognizing the multidimensional character of a teacher. It also sets the stage for teachers to try out the various options to professional development presented by the different models, those they are comfortable with and those that present more of a challenge. A multidimensional approach to staff development encourages teachers who might ordinarily be reluctant to try new approaches because not all of their eggs are in one basket. Teachers may not be equally successful in all areas of this multidimensional approach, but then, confronting differences is part of growing. Akin (1987) found that the most common and powerful experience associated with the need to know, and thus with the start of important learning, is actual failure. Real programs of professional development must be prepared to include and respect failure as the first step to self-discovery and the platform from which to try again. School districts that do this nourish the risk taking essential to the very best examples of professional development, and allowing teachers to combine models mollifies the potential for failure in a singular effort.

The downside of combining professional development models and setting objectives in several areas is that some teachers may be paralyzed by fear of failure before they have begun. These are teachers who, overwhelmed by the prospect of being challenged to do too much, will do nothing. The other side of the negative coin finds teachers who will spread themselves so thin trying to do too much that what they do will have no real quality or value. Perceptive and sensitive administrators can be vital mentors to teachers as they develop combination plans for professional growth, pointing out the need to develop growth plans that will prove feasible as well as productive.

Ideally, every teacher's professional growth plan should include a wide range of field activities and challenges. True individualization, however, requires that the plan also be sensitive to individual variations in response to growth diversification. Diversification is acceptable only as a means to an end, not an end in itself. The goal of professional development must be positive teacher growth in experience, reflection, and self-esteem, not frustration and defeat. The following discussion questions draw attention to some of the issues presented by combining professional development models.

Discussion Questions

1. What are some of the administrative drawbacks of combining professional development models?

2. Which models are most effectively combined?

3. How would you counsel a teacher who is trying to do too much?

4. Should an administrator have the authority to add to or delete elements of a teacher's professional growth plan? Why or why not?

5. Write an evaluation for an element of a combined staff development plan that has proven ineffective.

Activities

1. Create a professional growth plan for yourself that will involve three of the models studied, and describe how you will implement each part of your plan.

2. Develop a professional growth plan incorporating the research-focused and external career ladder formats.

3. Develop a professional growth plan incorporating the school improvement and internal career ladder formats.

4. Discuss how merit pay can be effectively linked to focused-training and focused-research staff development in a plan combining these professional growth models.

5. Interview your principal concerning the feasibility of a multi-faceted approach to professional growth.

6. Interview collective bargaining unit leaders concerning the feasibility of personalizing professional development through a multifaceted approach. What, if any, concerns do they have?

7. Interview collective bargaining unit leaders concerning their response to each of the specific professional development models presented. Which do they favor most? Which do they favor least? Why?

8. Summarize your own perspective on this approach to professional development. Which model(s) do you believe will make professional development a real and meaningful part of teaching?

Conferencing for Personalized Professional Growth

Effective conferencing with teachers is an important part of planning for personalized professional growth, and this conferencing should be both informal and formal. It takes place in five stages, each planned and executed by the administrator coordinating professional growth and individual teachers:

1. The preliminary personal review
2. The end-of-year planning conference
3. The initializing fall conference
4. The implementation progress conferences
5. The summary conference

These five conference steps define a conference cycle for planning personalized professional growth. That is, the summary report conference sets the stage for the preliminary personal review and all ensuing steps in each new school year of professional development. The purpose of each conference stage is discussed, and an outline of suggested activities and conference questions for each stage is presented.

Ideally, these conference stages should become an inherent part of the administrator's everyday schedule, not an accumulating duty left to build up to some contractual deadline. Effective personalized professional growth is integral to what teachers and administrators do every working day. Personalized professional growth is not a single event, a unique experience, a silver bullet. Personalized professional growth activities create a professional awareness continuum from the beginning to the end of the school year, every day in a teacher's life.

Step 1: The Preliminary Personal Review

During this conferencing stage, the administrator and the teacher get to know each other personally and professionally. Earlier, it was noted that each teacher was uniquely influenced by a vast array of personal, professional, and organizational factors and that the teacher's development needs would change depending on how factors in each of these arenas lined up to influence a teacher's professional need perception. In this preliminary conference step, the administrator developing professional growth plans must try to get a handle on the factors presently controlling each teacher's professional goals.

A combination of formal record review and informal conferences best serves this purpose. The administrator begins by noting such points as degrees held, certificates held, professional experience, and tenure status for each teacher. These factors should be part of an existing personnel record available from the district office for easy review. Informal conferencing comes through daily contact with individual teachers in classrooms, corridors, lunchrooms, and meetings. Informal conferencing is the process of getting to know the teachers in a building personally and becoming sensitive to the external pressures that will influence their professional development needs and expectations. Informal conferencing does not take place during scheduled office inquisitions. Informal conferencing is a by-product of unplanned, caring concern for what is having an effect on teachers' lives.

Administrative activities that can create a forum for informal conferencing include, but are not limited to,

1. Greeting teachers as they arrive for work each day
2. Being visible in corridors throughout the school day
3. Visiting each classroom each day for even a short time
4. Eating lunch in the teachers' lunchroom
5. Being certain to touch base with each teacher each day

Informal conferencing can be covered by a host of questions, but some good icebreakers include the following:

1. How are you doing today?
2. How's the family?
3. Are you feeling better? (To be used after a teacher's absence)
4. How's that course your taking?
5. What do you think about . . . ? (To be followed by any topic of current interest or concern)

This is by no means an exhaustive list of questions for informal conferencing, but these questions illustrate the personalized approach vital to this preliminary conference stage.

Step 2: The End-of-Year Planning Conference

It should be obvious that personalized professional growth requires a degree of planning that is at present foreign to professional development in public schools. To expedite this process, it is suggested that the actual conference at which models are selected and plans made take place at the end, not the beginning, of the school year. This will give the administrator in charge the summer to plan the details for implementing the more challenging personalized professional growth plans. It will also give the teacher time to plan, unpressured by the demands encountered with the start of the school year.

At this stage, the teacher and administrator review available models for professional growth, and they select an appropriate planning guide to formalize the procedures, timelines, and expected outcomes of the plan. Appropriate activities for this stage might include

1. A review of the models available for personalized professional growth
2. Review and possible revision of the planning guide to better reflect actual project goals and procedures
3. Completion of the planning guide
4. Development of an administrative plan for providing the teacher needed resources for successful implementation of the model

Some questions that might be pertinent to this conference are the following:

1. What model or models will you use this year?
2. Why have you chosen this model?
3. How must the suggested planning guide be adjusted?
4. What resources will you need?
5. When will you be ready to give a progress report?

This stage, the most time-consuming in the sequence, lies at the heart of successful implementation. It establishes the mechanics for carrying a personalized professional development plan forward and gives the administrator and teacher the summer months to iron out the details of implementation.

Step 3: The Initializing Fall Conference

If the end-of-year planning conference is done well, this conference becomes a mere perfunctory meeting to get the proverbial ball rolling. Objectives, timelines, and anticipated obstacles and outcomes are reviewed. Requested resources are provided, or adjustments are made to the original plan.

The activities preceding this stage of conferences include

1. Administrative review of the individual professional development plan
2. Resource review and provision
3. Scheduling of individual initiating conferences

Some appropriate questions for these conferences might be the following:

1. Are you ready to begin your personalized professional development activities?
2. Do you need any further resources?
3. Do you have any concerns about implementation?
4. When will you be ready to discuss progress made?

This stage of the cycle should involve a short, but formal, allotment of time to meet with individual teachers and activate the agreed-on plan of action.

Step 4: The Implementation Progress Conferences

Ideally, the administrator should check in with the teacher at least twice during the course of the project. These progress conferences should be nonthreatening efforts to assist the teacher by providing advice, resources, or simply a listening ear. Personalized professional development must be internalized to be effective, and these conferences are meant to help the teacher do this. They should not become external evaluations. To do so would defeat the process of being free to learn from experience.

Activities for this stage include

1. Personalized professional development plan review
2. A visit to the plan site
3. Written observations of the plan in effect
4. Formal or informal meetings with the teacher to discuss observations and plan progress

Administrative comments based on these observations might give rise to the following kinds of conference questions:

1. How do you feel the plan is progressing?
2. What obstacles and problems are you encountering?
3. What adjustments, if any, have you made to your plan?

These progress conferences need not be time-consuming or formal, but they should follow some form of direct observation of the plan in progress.

Step 5: The Summary Conference

This final review of each teacher's personal professional achievements should be the longest of the conferences planned. It will not be simply an end to the year's activities. It will also be a beginning, the time for planning ahead based on what has or has not been accomplished during the year reviewed. To prepare for this conference, the administrator should

1. Review a copy of the initial plan with any adjustments made as a result of the progress implementation conferences
2. Schedule adequate conference time with each teacher
3. Consider possible ways in which this year's plan can have an effect on next year's plan
4. Consider continued need and availability of resources
5. Review teacher's updated résumé and portfolio before conference

This is a very important stage in the successful implementation of personalized professional growth. It is a time for the teacher to reap the rewards, if any, of the process. At the very least, there should be a sense of achievement in carrying a project forward to completion. It is hoped that there will also be a sense of learning and fulfillment from the process. To assist the teacher in deriving both internal and external benefits from the experience, the administrator should make résumé and portfolio review an integral part of the process at this stage.

This culminating conference gives the teacher a reason for creating a tangible record of what has been accomplished. Based on this record, the administrator might ask specific questions relating to the project and the following general questions to gauge the project's personal effect on the teacher:

1. Do you feel the project was a success?
2. What did you find most rewarding about the project?
3. What did you find most frustrating about the project?
4. What, if anything, would you have done differently?
5. Can you use this project to plan for the coming year? If so, how would you use it?

Thus the cycle for one year's personalized professional growth sets the stage for the next. The summary conference evolves into the end-of-year planning conference and the potential for professional growth continues. Only this last summary and planning conference need be a lengthy, planned, and formal meeting. If done well, it allows subsequent conferences to become part of the fabric of school life, anticipated moments in an ongoing daily process of personalized professional growth.

12

Creating a Context for Personalized Professional Growth

The Principal's Role

Professional development is multidimensional. Leithwood (1990) notes that principals influence three dimensions of teacher development: development of professional expertise, psychological development, and career cycle development. He stresses the importance of attending to all three dimensions of teacher development and creating school cultures and structures hospitable to such development. To date, however, professional expertise alone has been the overwhelming focus of professional development. We have neglected teachers' psychological and career cycle development. We have failed to personalize the professional development experience.

The staff developer is a social architect whose goal is to build a culture of learning (Garmston, 1991). In reality, the principal must be the primary staff developer, because it is the principal who has the greatest direct control over the factors affecting school environment. Principals create the environments in which teachers teach and students learn, and they are ultimately responsible for all aspects of that evolving culture. They essentially create the context in which professional growth is either encouraged or suppressed. Contexts that nurture support and trust, encourage shared decision making and responsibility, and provide ongoing assistance and opportunities for problem solving appear best in sustaining successful improvement efforts (Guskey & Sparks, 1991b). Once individuals have exhausted their own mental and emotional resources, they are unlikely to be motivated to grow without the intervention of some external impetus (Duke & Stiggins, 1990). That external impetus usually comes from a supportive and creative building principal.

A variety of factors are needed for effective staff development, including a clear vision and goals, a multiyear process, strong instructional leadership, appropriate technical assistance, early success, sustained interaction among stakeholders, and staff development for everyone involved (Stringfeld, Billig, & Davis, 1991). The common denominator in attaining these factors is the principal, a manager of time, incentives, materials, and ethos. Leithwood (1990) believes effective principals use the energy and momentum created naturally by the demands of their work for purposes of teacher development. In essence, they redefine problems as solutions. An effective instructional leader is one who strategically applies knowledge to solve contextually specific problems and achieve the purposes of schooling through others (Krug, 1992). Solving these problems has a direct effect on the school's mission and an indirect, but equally significant, effect on the professional development of the teacher. Happy, productive staff members cannot but benefit students and vice versa (Raebeck, 1994).

The principal's role in nurturing professional growth begins with a sensitivity to individual teacher needs. Principals must truly *know* their teachers and develop a professional kinship with each one that goes beyond the annual evaluation visit or a cursory greeting in the hall. The best classes, the best schools, the best human enterprises combine high productivity with high sensitivity (Raebeck, 1994). This takes personal time and commitment but is central to bringing about real change.

Staff development, as it is presently carried out, makes it easy for individual principals and teachers to remain distant and uncommitted participants. Rarely is the inservice focus something either would have chosen themselves, and even more rarely is there any accountability for participation or actual implementation of the concept presented. In contrast, professional development goals and activities tailored by principals to individual teacher needs would create an innate demand for involvement and accountability on the part of both principal and teacher. All the old excuses disappear when principal and teacher sit down one-on-one to design a program of professional development.

Providing Time

Teachers need time to be actively involved in any one of the suggested models for professional development. There are, however, viable ways to secure time for what we consider important, and it is one of a principal's major responsibilities to clear away the major red herrings inhibiting real professional growth. Time is one such red herring, and the real issue may be not lack of time but better use of time already there (Loucks-Horsley et al., 1987). Time is especially important in a professional development plan that has teachers involved in daily individual activities as opposed to the usual, one-shot, large group scheduled activities. Nevertheless, if we break the bonds of tradition and allow more flexibility in both staffing and scheduling, time will not be a problem. Specific suggestions for providing time for personal professional growth follow.

Building administrators can substitute for classroom teachers. If each building administrator took over just one class period each day, at least one classroom teacher each day would have time to carry out a professional growth activity. The administrator would also have the opportunity for a professional growth experience in returning to the classroom and experiencing firsthand the demands of classroom teaching. Administrators who have been too long out of the classroom give validity to teacher skepticism regarding their ability to understand what goes on there. Administrators who regularly return to the classroom enhance their image as leaders.

Train and maintain an enrichment cadre of substitute teachers. This group of permanent substitute teachers would work with the administration and classroom teachers to provide special learning activities that relate to and enhance the existing curriculum. These teachers would be part of the school community, on most days either substituting for an absent teacher or working with teachers to plan for future professional development substitutions. For example, they could work with a class to present a play relating to a historical period being studied, create a showcase display of book reviews for an English class, or develop an interdisciplinary math project.

Employ one roving substitute to relieve teachers for professional development. This substitute teacher would work with the teachers in advance to establish what is to be taught and carry out the planned regular curriculum. Dedicated substitution could release at least one teacher each day for the express purpose of professional development. This dedicated long-term position should be specifically planned for in the substitute budget.

Encourage team teaching. Under this plan, teachers would work together with groups of students and would be capable of relieving each other as needed to conduct individual professional growth activities.

Develop a visiting artist, artisan, or expert program. Under this plan, large group demonstration and instruction would be provided as an enrichment activity. Students could be supervised by administrators, members of teaching teams, or substitutes, assisted by teacher aides or parent volunteers during the course of the program thereby freeing regular teachers for professional development.

Schedule special teachers to accommodate teachers' professional growth needs. This simply means scheduling time spent with art, music, PE, and other special subject area teachers to give regular classroom teachers optimum professional growth time. These classes lend themselves to large-group and extended block instruction with the assistance of aides, volunteers, or student teachers. If scheduled as a special subject area block, they can provide a significant period of time (often as much as a half day) for professional development activities.

Encourage cooperative research and articulation with a local university. Under this plan, the administrator would facilitate opportunities for university professors and teachers to exchange roles and collaborate on research, experiential lecturing, and presentations. Practicing classroom teachers have a great deal to contribute to university research and practice, and exchanges of a day or more at a time can provide release time for professional development.

Develop minisabbaticals for teachers. Here teachers proposing professional growth projects such as curriculum writing, professional writing, and retraining that would directly benefit the school environment would be provided funding where possible and be granted leave with impunity if funding is not available.

Replace unnecessary faculty meetings with released time for professional growth. Many times, faculty meetings simply amount to a list of announcements that could have been reduced to a brief written memo. If a planned meeting has no relevant and immediate purpose requiring that all faculty be present, it is a waste of time, one of many our educational rituals sustain. It would be far better to have teachers use the time to work on projects that are relevant and significant to their professional development.

Create opportunities for the exchange of professional opinion. A faculty lounge with coffee and donuts can be a place to gather to discuss an article on a controversial issue. An afterschool potluck dessert can be the setting for training. A professional library, well stocked and advertised, will provide a more formal environment for professional exchange. A professional newsletter highlighting current issues in education, as well as on-site research, and editorial comment on professional issues will also be a stimulus to professional discussion and inquiry.

Finding time for the principal to do all this. At about this point, principals are wondering where they will find the time to do all that personalizing professional growth required of them. This is one of the many demands placed on effective leaders, and response to it lies in referring back to research noted earlier in this chapter. Effective principals use the energy and momentum created naturally by the demands of their work for purposes of teacher development (Leithwood, 1990). In other words, letting qualified teachers help with the planning and implementation of these ideas is itself a form of productive professional development. The training of a cadre of substitute teachers or a roving substitute; the development of teaching teams; the securing of visiting artists, artisans, and experts; the block scheduling of special subject area teachers; the development of cooperative ties to a university; and the planning of events, places, and formats for professional exchange are all things that teachers can help principals do if given the time and fiscal support they may need. Teachers, however, do not control budgets and the allocation of resources.

Providing Resources

McLaughlin (1990) stresses the importance of strong support for teachers from both principals and superintendents, and providing tangible resources is central to such support. In addition to providing time for teachers to grow professionally, principals must also supply the material resources that support growth. These resources may include such tangibles as books, journals, videos, speakers, and travel allowances, as well as extrinsic incentives, stipends, and merit pay. In the final analysis, these are price tag items that require planned funding, but they should also be thought of as an investment in professional growth and school improvement.

Money, or more to the point, the lack of it, has always been a problem for educators. But it must not become an excuse for inertia. It is essential that the principal use traditional and creative ways to secure the dollars needed for effective professional development programs and projects. Like any other CEO, the principal must accept the raising of capital for development as an integral part of the administrative mission.

The following list includes traditional and novel ways to find the dollars needed. They are really a combination of planning, begging, and marketing in that they combine simply dedicating and asking for funds with some creative ways to secure them through business marketing strategies.

Make professional development a budget line item. If professional development is important, it must be provided for in the annual budget, and this line item should not be the first to go when cuts are made. Too often, professional development is viewed by a cost-cutting board as fat, a superfluous extra, because principals and unions simply do not fight for it. Professional development is not an extra. It is an essential whose place in the budget must be secured and defended. Although both budgeting and grantwriting have been traditional ways of securing funding, it is suggested that they be pursued with nontraditional fervor.

Research and write grants, and support teachers in their grantwriting efforts. In the case of grantwriting, schools should realize that there are dollars in both the private and public sector out there for the asking. Few school districts, however, provide either the subsidized salary for a full- or part-time grantwriter, or the released time for a teacher or administrator to do the job effectively. Doing the job effectively means researching grant sources, compiling data regarding the types of projects they fund, working with those to be involved in developing appropriate projects, completing the paperwork required, and submitting all materials within the established timelines. It also means following up on grants to understand why they are or are not funded and essentially developing an expertise in understanding what grant-funding sources are seeking. Unfortunately, schools are too often penny-wise and pound-foolish in the way they approach grantwriting, trying to fit it haphazardly into existing schedules and procedures, thus often missing the boat on securing this vital source of revenue.

Grantwriting could be an excellent career ladder opportunity for a teacher who would agree to teach part-time and be released part of the day to handle a school's grantwriting projects. Because the cost to administer a grant can be built into the grant itself, if successful, the grantwriter's salary could eventually be taken care of in the grants themselves. If a teacher is not available, there may be a parent volunteer eager to reenter the workforce who would act as a grantwriter at minimal or no cost to the school or district. The potential writer stands to gain firsthand experience in public relations, budgeting, and administration, all on a freelance basis not easily found in private sector employment, which seldom pays for untested talent. To help the neophyte grantwriter, there are usually foundation agencies in the community or courses at local universities that provide initial training, again at minimal or no cost to the district, for those interested in applying for grant funds. Foundation Center Library Services, disseminating current information on foundation and corporate giving, have offices in New York City, Washington, DC, Cleveland, San Francisco, and over 180 cooperating libraries in all 50 states. Through these library collections, grantwriters have access to a wide range of books, periodicals, and research documents relating to foundation giving and grant availability. The grantwriter, however, must have time and incentives to do the job as it should be done.

Grantwriting as it is presently done by school districts tends to be a haphazard and half-hearted attempt to shoot an arrow into the dark and hope it lands in the proverbial pot of gold. More often than not, it ends up a waste of time. If, however, schools and school districts would recognize that there is a method to this madness called grantwriting, that it is a learned skill that can be very rewarding for all involved, schools will begin to see grant funding as a realistic alternative funding source.

Seek the support of local businesses and service organizations for specific projects. Grantwriting is not the only funding source ineffectively tapped by schools. Fiscal support from local businesses, industries, and community groups is also approached in a haphazard fashion. Schools do little to mount public relations programs until tax levies need passage or bad press needs countering. In the interim, there are usually only lukewarm attempts to keep the public informed of what schools are doing, and even fewer attempts to invite them to join in our efforts. If schools operated like effective businesses, they would make public relations an integral part of what they do, not an afterthought. Support comes more willingly when those being asked see a *specific* need, are kept posted on progress, and are recognized publicly for their support and involvement in helping to address that need.

Once again, this approach requires a more concerted and controlled effort than schools presently give. Effective businesses have public relations liaisons, representatives who specifically create and nurture the corporate image in the community. Schools do not, but should. Such a position can be another rung in a career ladder for teachers, or a step up for an ambitious parent wishing to reenter the workforce on a part-time freelance basis or a principal who has and takes the time. It need not be an expensive proposition, but continuing to do nothing is.

A good public relations liaison writes the press releases on what schools are doing on a regular basis, arranges for public broadcasting visits, invites community groups to school-sponsored activities, publishes a school-community newsletter, arranges neighborhood coffees, fields controversy, and publicly recognizes community group and corporate cooperation and achievement. In short, a good public relations liaison builds the school's image in a community thereby laying the groundwork for continued fiscal and moral support for its mission. This is a challenging but rewarding job that remains unfilled in most school districts.

Establish ties with local universities and barter services. Universities provide another creative channel of indirect fiscal support for a school's professional development program. At present, rewards for university faculty in colleges of education are for studying teachers not for preparing them (Goodlad, 1990; Judge, 1982). On the contrary, schools and universities need to change and become partners in both study and preparation. Working together, they can tailor professional development and research to site needs. The important thing for schools to realize in their relations with local universities is that public schools have something important to give to universities. They are the only legitimate laboratories the universities' colleges of education have, and no research or theory can be taken seriously until effectively tested within the public school classroom. With this bargaining chip in hand, public school administrators should barter with universities for services related to professional development and school improvement research. Clark and Hood (1986) describe how the University of Vermont developed a program in which teachers can earn master's degrees through course work directly responding to school improvement projects. Teachers take courses at school sites, and the university provides the technical assistance needed to identify school needs and develop courses and programs addressing those needs. Such collaboratives are valuable untapped resources that can benefit schools and universities, and breach the gap between research and practice.

Develop professional growth collaboratives with other schools. Another version of professional development cooperation that can allay expenses involves forming public school professional development collaboratives, building fiscal strength with numbers. Under this plan, a number of small or underfunded schools or school districts join together and pool their fiscal resources to be able to afford and share nationally recognized trainers, speakers, materials, and funded programs. Cooperatively, they select a convenient neutral site or take turns hosting the selected programs and housing resources.

Publish and market products of professional development. A final untapped resource for supporting professional development in both spirit and substance is the marketing of professional materials and programs developed internally. Talented teachers are doing good things in their classrooms every day, but often they do not have the opportunity to share their ideas in the educational marketplace. Enterprising and creative school administrators can help teachers and schools by establishing publishing and production ties that will help disseminate and market worthwhile materials. In addition, teachers should be encouraged to make presentations and participate in teaching craft fairs where ideas and hands-on materials can be demonstrated and purchased. Schools, as other businesses that foster development on the job, can legitimately share in the fiscal profits of such a venture with the understanding that all such profits will be rolled back into the support of future professional development efforts.

Creating Ethos

Ethos is the disposition, character, or fundamental values peculiar to a specific group, culture, or movement. Every school has an ethos for which the principal is primarily responsible. The principal is the instructional leader and in that capacity sets the professional expectations for the school and creates a climate to sustain these expectations. As discussed, there are a variety of factors that create the expectation and recognition of professionalism. The essential component in any process of transformation is attitude, although finances and resources—or the lack of them—are used as an excuse for maintaining the status quo (Raebeck, 1994). A principal's attitude toward professional development is defined by what the principal does to make professional development important.

Principals must be well read, informed, and professionally involved. Central to an ethos of professionalism is the principal's own commitment to personal professional growth and improvement. A good principal is a well-read, informed, and involved professional, a living resource for staff, students, and parents. A good principal is a professional exemplar fostering this same sense of involved and informed professionalism throughout the school community.

Principals must personalize conferencing concerning professional growth. Perhaps the most important step a principal must take in creating an ethos for professional growth is that of getting to know teachers as individuals with unique talents, needs, and concerns. Far too many principals isolate themselves from their staffs. It is so easy to sacrifice the human element of leadership to the time-consuming mechanics of the process—to put scheduling before classroom visitation, phone calls before meetings with individuals, a working lunch behind a closed office door before the collegial exchange one finds in the teacher's cafeteria. If, however, principals are to have any real and lasting effect on teachers, they must dispel the image of an isolated and uncaring administration and spend quality time getting to know the teachers in the building. Every plan for professional growth begins with a needs assessment, a method of discovering the gaps between what "is" and what "ought" to take place in schools (Orlich, 1989). To help a teacher plan for effective individual growth, a principal must first know where the teacher is.

Principals must actively foster professional discussion and collaboration. Teachers must be given opportunities for professional exchange. Successful staff development efforts require a substantial amount of ownership, participation, and time for participants (Levine & Broude, 1989). The monthly faculty meeting does not meet this need. In fact, such large meetings, with agendas better covered in written memos, often work to further isolate the teacher by ignoring individual needs and concerns. It would be far better to use this time for structured small group discussion and team planning. Impromptu teas and coffees, brown bag luncheons, retreats, and planned released times can be used to facilitate such better interaction. A study group is also an opportunity for teachers to think through their own beliefs, share ideas, challenge current educational practices, blend theory and practice, and identify professional and personal needs (Matlin & Short, 1991). Such sharing, exchange, and challenge are central, not peripheral, to the development of a professional identity.

Principals must actively develop merit pay and career ladders for teachers. Incentives for involvement increase commitment (Hirsh & Ponder, 1991). Incentives for teachers, however, are presently few and far between. Education continues to dull the competitive edge needed to make it a true profession that recognizes differentiated skill and achievement. It will take creative and bold administrators to change the status quo and give teachers such real growth opportunities. Merit pay financially rewards quality in teaching, and several school districts and teachers unions are moving in this direction. In Cincinnati, for example, the board and the Cincinnati Federation of Teachers have agreed to a 3-year contract linking a teacher's advancement on the salary scale to performance (A. Bradley, 1994). Essentially, merit pay recognizes that not all teachers are the same. Some simply do a better job than others, and they are rewarded accordingly.

Career ladders, in contrast, reward teachers for doing more. Teachers who take on assignments outside of the classroom are fiscally rewarded for their willingness to do so. Career ladders create opportunities for teachers to work as professional educators in new and challenging ways that serve the best interests of the school, the district, and the individuals. Districts have ignored the practical knowledge of their staff and have shunned perhaps their greatest chances for success (Lambert, 1988). Teachers can take on new roles as program coordinators, community liaisons, editors, curriculum developers, mentors, and staff developers. Districts not only benefit from the practical knowledge of their own professionals, participants prefer learning from their peers, and programs are more easily customized to meet local needs and priorities (Britton, 1989).

In summary, principals create an ethos supportive of professional development by making such development an essential part of their own lives as well as the lives of their teachers. Only by making a personal investment of time, energy, resources, and reputation will principals succeed in taking the risks needed to make the concept of professional development meaningful in their schools.

The Staff Developer's Role

Principals, as instructional leaders, are the best staff developers. In large schools (faculty over 50), however, it may be difficult for a principal to do all that a good staff development manager should do and attend to the other day-to-day demands of building management as well. When this is the case, a staff development position should be created, and the staff developer should be responsible for planning

and administering the programs and procedures discussed throughout this book. To be effective, the staff developer must have both the
authority and responsibility to make decisions regarding individual
professional development plans and the budgetary freedom to fund
their implementation. The staff developer should be the principal's
chief adviser and representative in staff development matters.

Actual qualifications for the position of staff developer should
include

- Master's degree (minimum)
- Formal course work in the areas of testing and measurement,
  statistics, curriculum, and supervision
- A minimum of 5 years' teaching experience at the instructional
  level of the staff development assignment
- Evidence of good communication skills
- Experience in planning and implementing long-range programs
- Experience in budget management and planning
- Evidence of good public relations skills
- Evidence of creative program development
- Experience in evaluating program outcomes

Ideally, the position of staff developer should be one requiring certification based on field experience in the area. Staff developers must
have a good grasp of theory, but they must also be pragmatic imple-
menters with good people, public relations, and budgetary skills. This is
a very important and organizationally sensitive position, in that the
staff developer holds the future of the organization in hand. Staff
developers are the field of education's research and product development equivalents in the business world. An effective staff developer
will give the school a bright and productive future. An ineffective
staff developer will destroy individual and organizational initiative
thereby destroying any hope for future organizational productivity.

At present, there are no certification requirements for the position
of staff developer, and so inept charlatans, or well-intentioned, under-
paid, overbooked, and unprepared neophytes, sometimes fill the
void. In either case, they do more harm than good and continue the
tradition of wasted time and wasted money that educators have come
to equate with staff development. If we are serious about professional
development, staff developers should be accorded administrative

status and held accountable for program development, implementation, and evaluation.

As a profession, we should see the administrative role of staff developer as a new job opportunity for educators, another way in which educators who want to do something other than teach can choose to direct their careers. Management of staff development is a supervisory role that should require training and field experience in public relations, administrative planning, budgeting, school law, educational statistics and measurement, and curriculum. It should be a line position within the educational organization, that is, a position with authority to make decisions and the responsibility for the effect of those decisions.

The focus on professional development is most obvious in the Bush administration's Goals 2000: Educate America Act and in proposals for the Elementary and Secondary Education Act (ESEA; see A. Bradley, 1994). The Education Department's proposals for reauthorizing the ESEA heavily stress professional development, calling for it to become a vehicle for reform. If this legislative emphasis is to be more than mere rhetoric, there must be a concomitant commitment of funds and personnel to this focus. The appointment of an experienced and certified staff developer must become the rule, not the exception to the rule, in staffing for professional growth.

The Superintendent's Role

The superintendent is the board of education's official representative and adviser. As such, superintendents have great authority as well as responsibility for the course of a district's programs. Superintendents have the dual powers of purse and persuasion. That is, they have the direct ability to influence which programs a board of education will support and which they will not. Thus it could be argued that the superintendent has ultimate control of a district's and a school's plan for professional development. Although principals can still do much at the building level to foster professional growth in spite of a superintendent's disinterest, it is easier to foster professional development with the superintendent's clear and visible support.

Wise superintendents realize that concern for professional development is an investment in labor relations as well as program. Successful professional development sends the clear message to teachers that they are important to the organization they serve. Support of personalized professional growth opportunities is a visible statement that management cares, and it sets the stage for an equally caring response from faculty.

In addition, wise superintendents realize that professional development is the only way to successfully achieve necessary change in a district. It is an essential part of the big picture and the long-range plan. People will not change unless they see change as a way to improve their personal status quo, and this is the role of personalized professional growth plans. Thus superintendents must use personalized professional growth planning as a means to the end of effective district management.

Superintendents must provide inservices to the board on the value of professional development. Superintendents, like principals, must make professional development a priority in the district, a priority with a dedicated budget line. To do this, the superintendent should arrange for board members to see what effective professional development can do for the district. Professional development presentations, media recognition of teacher professional development efforts, and establishment of a visible connection between professional development and district goals are ways to do this. If teachers have developed a new curriculum, or are implementing new teaching techniques, this is an excellent opportunity to have them demonstrate these new approaches at a board meeting. If teachers attend conferences, get advanced degrees, engage in university exchanges, write books and articles, or travel, media coverage should be used to regularly highlight their accomplishments. If a district is considering the adoption of a new model for discipline or delivery of services, teachers engaged in the school improvement model of professional development should work with the board to study, review, evaluate, and finally decide approaches most suitable for the district. In other words, superintendents should stop treating professional development as a budget category that has no direct relationship to the district's goals and image. Professional development should become a visible and necessary means to the end of school improvement.

Superintendents must work with unions to make personalized professional growth opportunities possible. Superintendents will also have a primary role in working either directly or indirectly with the collective bargaining agent to negotiate ways in which professional development can be personalized. Unions exist to protect the collective interest. Personalized professional development requires that they also work to assist the individual teacher in attaining satisfying career objectives and goals. This will involve negotiating ways in which more progressive forms of professional development such as merit pay and internal and external career ladders can become equitable options. Superintendents willing to engage in collaborative or interest-based bargaining can work with unions to develop acceptable ways to implement these new approaches.

The Union's Role

Teachers unions also have an undeniable effect on the professional development of their membership. In many states, by law, wages, hours, and terms and conditions of employment must be negotiated in districts where teachers have designated a collective bargaining agent. Unions negotiate for the collective welfare of those they represent and work to achieve equity in all employment practices. This goal, however, often sacrifices individual need to the collective good. The concept of personalizing professional development can be a challenge to this traditional stance, but it need not be an insurmountable obstacle to professional development progress. After all, the end goal of all union activity is to do what is best for the membership, to maximize opportunity and minimize dissatisfaction with the work environment.

Classroom-centered and focused-training staff development can still be contractual vehicles for assisting teachers who have problems in the classroom. However, teachers with no pressing pedagogical problems should be allowed to choose from the options presented. The union's role in this process would be to assure that administration of the procedures used to implement each model is fair and equitable. In the case of more progressive models, such as the internal and external career ladders and merit pay, the procedures for selection and award should be negotiable terms of the employment contract that assure all teachers an equal opportunity for selection. These negotiated terms, however, should not ignore the fact that teachers are all different, with distinct needs and abilities, and that choices based on valid and negotiated criteria will have to be made.

If teachers unions are to be true professional organizations, they must acknowledge and support the professional diversity of their membership in the same way that the American Bar Association and the American Medical Association acknowledge the professional diversity of their members. These organizations do so by supporting and monitoring personalized opportunities for growth offered their constituents.

Monitoring Professional Growth

One key element presently missing in professional growth plans for teachers is a personal and professional record of that growth. There certainly are forms, administrative instruments, designed to document accountability, but rarely are teachers taught how to develop marketable records of their growth or, for that matter, given any reason to do so. This oversight gives a subliminal message that there is no place to really go once one becomes a classroom teacher. At best, there may be some mention of résumé writing in a final graduate practicum course. What is left unsaid is that an integral and ongoing part of career development *is* regularly updating one's résumé to reflect recent accomplishments. This exercise, conducted annually, can have both practical and professionally therapeutic benefits. On the practical side, it serves as a professional checkpoint. The teacher must review the year's accomplishments to update the résumé. In the process, the teacher has the opportunity to pause, reflect, and plan for future growth. There is a definite need for such reflection-in-practice (Schon, 1987), and it is an earmark of true professionalism. Reflection is a necessary first step in professional growth and improvement (McLaughlin & Pfeifer, 1988). Careers are planned. They do not simply happen. Résumé updating gives the teacher a focal point for looking back and planning ahead. Individuals who demonstrate a proclivity for continued growth seem to be more future oriented than others (Duke & Stiggins, 1990). Résumé updating need not be spurred only by the need for a new position. True professionals have an updated résumé always at hand as a tool in the general process of self-evaluation, a gauge of where one has been and where one is going.

A good résumé update is the official summary of a portfolio actually documenting professional growth activities for the year. Every practicing teacher should have a portfolio, file folder, or three-ring binder to hold the agendas, memos, responses, certificates, diplomas, and awards garnered as the result of professional involvement in a given year. An annual portfolio record reviewed in updating the résumé serves the purpose of giving the teacher a sense of accomplishment and esteem, not easily found in routine teaching. Keeping a portfolio provides teachers something concrete to admire, a discipline for assembling the evidence, and an occasion for doing so (Bird, 1990). The need for achievement and self-esteem may be a key variable in explaining individual differences in response to challenge (Locke, Shaw, Saari, & Latham, 1981).

On the practical side, processes for hiring, assigning, tenuring, evaluating, and taking other personnel actions should employ a range of pertinent evidence to reach fair and valid decisions (Bird, 1990). Portfolio assessment can serve this purpose thereby proving a benefit to the district as well as the teacher. Such a future-oriented approach may actually create a proclivity for continued growth by forcing teachers to regularly take stock of their professional status.

Many universities use such an approach in conducting their annual reviews of faculty performance. Faculty members prepare for annual reviews by carrying out self-assessments related to performance objectives and the institution's expectations (Bortz, 1987). A cycle is initiated that ends each academic year with a supervisory conference for the purpose of evaluating outcomes attained versus outcomes desired and planning goals for the next academic year (Creswell, Wheeler, Seagren, Egly, & Kirk, 1990). Faculty present evidence of growth, which is used to determine pay increases as well as rank and tenure decisions. Promotion and tenure require that the faculty member show evidence supporting quality of teaching; scholarship (publications, presentations, research contributions); and service to university, profession, or community (Tracy & MacNaughton, 1993). Although the purpose of the university approach is primarily assessment, reward giving, and faculty accountability (Bortz, 1987; Creswell et al., 1990), the process also sets the stage for the personal and professional reflection now ignored in most public school evaluation plans for teachers. The personalized professional portfolio should be the crowning touch in creating a context for effective professional growth in the public schools.

Summary

In a recent study, McBride (1994) assessed teacher attitudes toward staff development in a random sample of 500 teachers. Over half of the respondents (52.7%) said that staff development activities often lacked relevancy. Just over one third (38%) reported training applicable to their teaching, and only 36.9% believed that the activities provided them with new and creative ideas. Seventy percent of the respondents agreed that teacher commitment would be stronger if more teachers were involved in the planning process, and nearly 40% disagreed that staff development needs were identified by teachers. This is the current teacher perception of staff development programs despite recommendations that staff development programs be based on teacher interests and that staff developers need to survey teachers to obtain general consensus about topics (Nicholas, 1989). McBride found that teachers' needs continue to be ignored. It is the theory of this book that dissatisfaction with the current prescription for delivery of staff development continues because consensus about topics is not the complete answer. The real and complete answer rests with totally individualized professional growth plans—an approach built on the theory of different strokes for different folks.

Maslow's (1987) theory of motivation contends that people progress through a hierarchy of human needs—from needs for basic physical requirements, to safety, to affiliation, to esteem, to self-actualization. L. G. Katz (1985) identified three stages in teacher development: survival, consolidation, and renewal. B. Wood (1980) has distinguished between pedagogical models of instruction, primarily transmitting theories of education, and "andragogical" models of instruction, stimulating the learner's desire to know. This body of research and that cited throughout the book suggest to staff developers that some approaches to teaching teachers will be more successful than others and that the content of instruction suitable for teachers will vary as a function of the stage of their career (M. K. Bradley, Kallick, & Regan, 1991) in concert with personal, family, and organizational factors that uniquely combine and change (see Figure 1.1).

One of the strongest positions taken by teachers at the recent Goals 2000 Teacher Forum was their condemnation of "silver bullet" types of staff development. Teachers are trained professionals on differentiated career paths. As such, they deserve diversified, challenging learning experiences and opportunities. A system of professional development that acknowledges and builds on this professional diversity is the only real way to assure progress in the field of education. Recognizing individual professional need is also the only way to assure teacher cooperation and commitment to any organizational change effort. The emphasis must be on personal professional growth rather than staff development.

School improvement lies ultimately in people improvement (Hirsh & Ponder, 1991), but people are different, and their unique stages of development and need cannot be ignored. Professional development is teachers, administrators, classified staff, and resource personnel, all learning together in self-reflective and creative ways that ultimately make the school experience richer for students (Garmston, 1991). It is unlikely that any one program of professional growth can ever address the needs of such a vast and diverse group; nor should it. Diversity is an inherent part of real professionalism. Diversity, properly nourished, is the catalyst of creativity. Our present approach to staff development subverts diversity and discourages individuality while claiming to enhance professionalism. This is an oxymoron. Until individuality is not only recognized but nurtured, teaching will not be a true profession. And until teaching becomes more of a profession, it is unreasonable to expect the field to attract a sufficient number of talented individuals to public schools (Schlechty & Vance, 1983). The end result is perpetuation of an enervating cycle of mindless mediocrity.

Teachers themselves may be the only force to stop this cycle. They must play an active, not reactive, role in recapturing their professional identity. Teachers must claim their right to true professionalism with its inherent tenet of self-determination. In their dealings with both union and administration, good teachers must become more aggressive about what they need to become real professionals (Lewis, 1994).

Today's public schools are wells of untapped potential. To reach their potential for excellence, they should take a cue from the basic principles guiding America's top companies. They must provide for autonomy and entrepreneurship within the ranks and recognize that productivity comes through people (Peters & Waterman, 1982). Personalizing professional growth is a significant step in this direction.

References

Acheson, K., & Gall, M. (1992). *Techniques in the clinical supervision of teachers.* New York: Longman.

Akin, G. (1987). Varieties of managerial learning. *Organizational Dynamics, 16,* 36-48.

Albert, L. (1989). *A teacher's guide to cooperative discipline.* Circle Pines, MN: Ames Guidance Service.

Bacharach, S., Conley, S., & Shedd, J. (1990). Evaluating teachers for career awards and merit pay. In J. Millman & L. Darling-Hammond (Eds.), *The new handbook of teacher evaluation* (pp. 133-146). Newbury Park, CA: Sage.

Bennett, B. (1987). *The effectiveness of staff development training practices: A meta-analysis.* Unpublished doctoral dissertation, University of Oregon, Eugene, OR.

Bird, T. (1990). The schoolteacher's portfolio: An essay on possibilities. In J. Millman & L. Darling-Hammond (Eds.), *The new handbook of teacher evaluation* (pp. 241-255). Newbury Park, CA: Sage.

Bloom, B. S. (Ed.). (1956). *Taxonomy of educational objectives: The classification of educational goals. Handbook 1: Cognitive domain.* New York: David McKay.

Bortz, R. F. (1987). *Recognizing faculty contribution.* Carbondale, IL: Training Systems Designers.

Boyan, N. J., & Copeland, W. D. (1978). *Instructional supervision training program.* Columbus, OH: Merrill.

Bradley, A. (1994, July 13). Teacher training a key focus for administration. *Education Week, 13*(42), 4.

Bradley, A. (1995). Dallas to pilot-test teacher evaluation system. *Education Week, 14*(33), 3.

Bradley, M. K., Kallick, B. O., & Regan, H. B. (1991). *The staff development manager: A guide to professional growth.* Boston: Allyn & Bacon.

Britton, N. (1989, May). Training of trainers in Richardson, Texas. *The Developer.* 1, 3, 7.

Calhoun, E. F. (1993). Action research: Three approaches. *Educational Leadership, 51*(2), 62-65.

Canfield, J. (1986). *Self-esteem in the classroom.* Pacific Palisades, CA: Self-Esteem Seminars.

Canter, L., & Canter, M. (1989). *Assertive discipline.* Santa Monica, CA: Lee Canter & Associates.

Clark, J., & Hood, K. (1986). School improvement in a rural state. *Educational Leadership, 44*(1), 77-80.

Cochran-Smith, M., & Lytle, S. L. (1990). Research on teaching and teacher research: The issues that divide. *Educational Researcher, 19*(2), 2-11.

Costa, A. L., & Kallick, B. (1993). Through the lens of a critical friend. *Educational Leadership, 51*(2), 49-51.

Creswell, J. W., Wheeler, D. W., Seagren, A. T., Egly, N., & Kirk, D. B. (1990). *The academic chairperson's handbook.* Lincoln: University of Nebraska Press.

Cuban, L. (1990). Reforming again, again, and again. *Educational Researcher, 19*(1), 3-13.

Darling-Hammond, L. (1986). Teacher evaluation: A proposal. *Elementary School Journal, 86,* 531-551.

Doyle, W., & Ponder, G. (1977). The practical ethic and teacher decision-making. *Interchange, 8*(3), 1-12.

Duckett, W. R. (1984, April). Learning about merit pay from business and industry. *Phi Delta Kappa Research Bulletin.*

Duke, D. L., & Stiggins, R. J. (1990). Beyond minimum competence: Evaluation for professional development. In J. Millman & L. Darling-Hammond (Eds.), *The new handbook of teacher evaluation* (pp. 116-133). Newbury Park, CA: Sage.

Dunn, R., & Dunn, K. (1978). *Teaching students through their individual learning styles: A practical approach.* Reston, VA: Reston Publishing.

Fessler, R., & Christensen, J. (1992). *The teacher career cycle: Understanding and guiding the professional development of teachers.* Boston: Allyn & Bacon.

Flanders, N. A. (1970). *Analyzing teaching behavior.* Reading, MA: Addison-Wesley.

Gable, R., & Rogers, V. (1987). Taking the terror out of research. *Phi Delta Kappan, 68*, 690-695.

Gage, N. (1984). What do we know about teaching effectiveness? *Phi Delta Kappan, 66*, 87-93.

Garmston, R. J. (1987). How administrators support peer coaching. *Educational Leadership, 44*(5), 4-11.

Garmston, R. J. (1991). Staff developers as social architects. *Educational Leadership, 49*(3), 64-65.

Garmston, R. J., Linder, C., & Whitaker, J. (1993). Reflections on cognitive coaching. *Educational Leadership, 51*(2), 57-61.

Geis, A. A. (1987, January). Making merit pay work. *Personnel,* pp. 52-60.

Glatthorn, A. A. (1987). Cooperative professional development: Peer-centered options for teacher growth. *Educational Leadership, 45*(3), 31-35.

Glickman, C. (1986). Developing teacher thought. *Journal of Staff Development, 7*(1), 6-21.

Glickman, C. (1990). *Supervision of instruction: A developmental approach* (2nd ed.). Boston: Allyn & Bacon.

Goldenberg, C., & Gallimore, R. (1991, April). *Teaching and learning in a new key: The instructional conversation.* Paper presented at the annual meeting of the American Educational Research Association, Chicago.

Goodlad, J. I. (1990). Better teachers for our nation's schools. *Phi Delta Kappan, 72*, 187.

Guskey, T. R. (1986). Staff development and the process of teacher change. *Educational Researcher, 15*(5), 5-12.

Guskey, T. R. (1990). Integrating Innovations. *Educational Leadership, 47*(5), 11-15.

Guskey, T. R., & Sparks, D. (1991a, April). *Complexities in evaluating the effects of staff development programs.* Paper presented at the annual meeting of the American Educational Research Association, Chicago.

Guskey, T. R., & Sparks, D. (1991b). What to consider when evaluating staff development. *Educational Leadership, 49*(3), 73-76.

Hall, G. E., Loucks, S. F., Rutherford, W. L., & Newlove, B. N. (1975). Levels of use of the innovation: A framework for analyzing innovation adoption. *Journal of Teacher Education, 26*(1), 52-56.

Hange, J. (1982, March). *Teachers in their fifth year: An analysis of teaching concerns from the perspectives of adult and career development.* Paper presented at the annual meeting of the American Educational Research Association, New York.

Helmer, O. (1967). *Analysis of the future: The Delphi method.* Santa Monica, CA: RAND.

Hirsh, S., & Ponder, G. (1991). New plots, new heroes in staff development. *Educational Leadership, 49*(3), 44.

Hunter, M. (1984). Knowing, teaching, and supervising. In P. Hosford (Ed.), *Using what we know about teaching* (pp. 169-192). Alexandria, VA: Association for Supervision and Curriculum Development.

Ingvarson, L., & Greenway, P. (1981). *Portrayals of teacher development.* Washington, DC. (ERIC Document Reproduction Service No. ED 200 600)

Iwanicki, E. F. (1990). Teacher evaluation for school improvement. In J. Millman & L. Darling-Hammond (Eds.) *The new handbook of teacher evaluation* (pp. 158-171). Newbury Park, CA: Sage.

Johnson, D. W., & Johnson, R. T. (1987). Research shows the benefits of adult cooperation. *Educational Leadership, 45*(3), 27-30.

Johnson, R. W. (1993). Where can teacher research lead? One teacher's daydream. *Educational Leadership, 51*(2), 66-68.

Joyce, B., & McKibbin, M. (1982). Teacher growth states and school environments. *Educational Leadership, 40*(2), 36-41.

Joyce, B., & Showers, B. (1988). *Student achievement through staff development.* New York: Longman.

Judge, H. (1982). *American graduate schools of education.* New York: Ford Foundation.

Katz, D., & Kahn, R. L. (1978). *The social psychology of organizations* (2nd ed.). New York: John Wiley.

Katz, L. G. (1985). Research currents: Teachers as learners. *Language Arts, 62,* 778-782.

Keith, S., & Girling, R. H. (1991). *Education, management, and participation.* Boston: Allyn & Bacon.

Knowles, M. (1980). *The modern practice of adult education.* Chicago: Association/Follett.

Knowles, M. (1984). *Andragogy in action.* San Francisco: Jossey-Bass.

Knowles, M. (1986). *Using learning contracts: Practical approaches to individualizing and structuring learning.* San Francisco: Jossey-Bass.

Knox, A. B. (1977). *Adult development and learning.* San Francisco: Jossey-Bass.

Knox, A. B. (1986). *Helping adults learn.* San Francisco: Jossey-Bass.

Kouzes, J. M., & Posner, B. Z. (1990). *The leadership challenge: How to get extraordinary things done in organizations.* San Francisco: Jossey-Bass.

Krug, S. E. (1992). Instructional leadership: A constructivist perspective. *Educational Administration Quarterly, 28,* 430-443.

Lambert, L. (1988). Staff development redesigned. *Phi Delta Kappan, 69,* 665-668.

Leithwood, K. A. (1990). The principal's role in teacher development. In B. Joyce (Ed.), *Changing school culture through staff development* (pp. 71-90). Alexandria, VA: Association for Supervision and Curriculum Development.

Levine, S. (1989). *Promoting adult growth in schools.* Boston: Allyn & Bacon.

Levine, S., & Broude, N. (1989). Designs for learning. In S. Caldwell (Ed.), *Staff development: A handbook of effective practices* (pp. 70-83). Oxford, OH: National Staff Development Council.

Lewis, A. C. (1994). Developing good staff development. *Phi Delta Kappan, 75*(7), 509.

Lieberman, A. (1986). Collaborative research: Working with, not working on. *Educational Leadership, 43*(5), 28-32.

Lier, J., & Bufe, B. (1993). Quantum leap—A teacher and a consultant exchange jobs. *Educational Leadership, 51*(2), 26-28.

Lipton, L. (1993, April). *Transforming information into knowledge: Structured reflection in administrative practice.* Paper presented at the annual meeting of the American Educational Research Association, Atlanta, GA.

Locke, E. A., Shaw, K. N., Saari, L. M., & Latham, G. P. (1981). Goal setting and task performance: 1969-1980. *Psychological Bulletin, 90,* 125-152.

Loucks-Horsley, S., Harding, C. K., Arbuckle, M. A., Murray, L. B., Dubea, C., & Williams, M. K. (1987). *Continuing to learn: A guidebook for teacher development.* Oxford, OH: National Staff Development Council.

Maehr, M. L., Midgley, C., & Urdan, T. (1992). School leader as motivator. *Educational Administration Quarterly, 28,* 410-429.

Maslow, A. H. (1987). A theory of human motivation. In J. M. Shafritz & A. C. Hyde (Eds.), *Classics of public administration* (pp. 80-95). Pacific Grove, CA: Brooks/Cole.

Matlin, M., & Short, K. G. (1991). How our teacher study group sparks change. *Educational Leadership, 49*(3), 68.

McBride, R. E. (1994). Teacher attitudes toward staff development: A symbolic relationship at best. *Journal of Staff Development, 15*(2), 37.

McKay, J. A. (1992). Professional development through action research. *Journal of Staff Development, 13*(1), 18-21.

McLaughlin, M. W. (1990). The Rand Change Agent Study revisited: Macro perspectives and micro realities. *Educational Researcher, 19*(9), 11-16.

McLaughlin, M. W., & Pfeifer, R. S. (1988). *Teacher evaluation: Improvement, accountability, and effective learning.* New York: Teachers College Press.

Murphy, J. (1987). Teacher evaluation: A conceptual framework for supervisors. *Journal of Personnel Evaluation in Education, 1,* 157-180.

National Commission on Excellence in Education. (1983). *A nation at risk: The imperative for educational reform.* Washington, DC: U.S. Department of Education.

National Science Board Commission on Precollege Education in Mathematics, Science, and Technology. (1983). *Educating Americans for the 21st century: A plan of action for improving mathematics, science and technology education for all American elementary and secondary students so that their achievement is the best in the world by 1995. A report to the American people and the National Science Board.* Washington, DC: National Science Board, National Science Foundation.

Newman, K. K., Burden, P. R., & Applegate, J. H. (1980a). Adult development is implicit in staff development. *Journal of Staff Development, 1*(2), 7-56.

Newman, K. K., Burden, P. R., & Applegate, J. H. (1980b, February). *Helping teachers examine their long range development.* Paper presented at the annual Association of Teacher Educators Conference, Washington, DC.

Nicholas, E. (1989). How to keep an aging teacher alive. *Principal, 69*(2), 27-28.

Oja, S. N., & Smulyan, L. (1989). *Collaborative action research: A developmental approach.* New York: Falmer.

Orlich, D. C. (1989). *Staff development: Enhancing human potential.* Boston: Allyn & Bacon.

Parker, J. C. (1985). *Career ladder/master teacher programs: Implications for principals.* Reston, VA: National Association of Secondary School Principals.

Peters, T. J., & Waterman, R. H. (1982). *In search of excellence: Lessons from America's best-run companies.* New York: Harper & Row.

Raebeck, B. (1994). The school as a humane business. *Phi Delta Kappan, 75*(10), 761-765.

Rebore, R. W. (1991). *Personnel administration in education: A management approach.* Englewood Cliffs, NJ: Prentice-Hall.

Riegle, R. P. (1987). Conceptions of faculty development. *Educational Theory, 37,* 53-59.

Robbins, P., & Wolfe, P. (1987). Reflections on a Hunter-based staff development project. *Educational Leadership, 44*(5), 56-61.

Robbins, S. P. (1982). *Personnel: The management of human resources* (2nd ed.). Englewood Cliffs, NJ: Prentice-Hall.

Rogers, C. (1969). *Freedom to learn.* Columbus, OH: Merrill.

Rosenshine, B. (1986). Synthesis of research on explicit teaching. *Educational Leadership, 43*(7), 60-68.

Rosenshine, B., & Furst, N. (1973). The use of direct observation to study teaching. In R. Travers (Ed.), *Handbook of research on teaching* (2nd ed., pp. 122-183). Chicago: Rand McNally.

Rudduck, J. (1989). Practitioner research and programmes of initial teacher education. *Westminster Studies in Education, 12,* 61-72.

Ryan, K., Flora, R., Newman, K., Peterson, A., Burden, P., & Mager, J. (1979, March). *The stages in teaching: New perspectives on staff development for teachers' needs.* Paper presented to the Association for Supervision and Curriculum Development, Anaheim, CA.

Schlechty, P., & Vance, B. (1983). Recruitment, selection, and retention: The shape of the teaching force. *Elementary School Journal, 83,* 469-487.

Schon, D. A. (1987). *Educating the reflective practitioner.* San Francisco: Jossey-Bass.

Sizer, T. (1992). *Horace's school: Redesigning the American high school.* Boston: Houghton Mifflin.

Sparks, D. (1983). Synthesis of research on staff development for effective teaching. *Educational Leadership, 41*(3), 65-72.

Sparks, D., & Loucks-Horsley, S. F. (1990). *Five models of staff development*. Oxford, OH: National Staff Development Council.

Sparks, D., & Simon, J. (1989). Inquiry-oriented staff development: Using research as a source of tools, not rules. In S. Caldwell (Ed.), *Staff development: A handbook of effective practices* (pp. 126-139). Oxford, OH: National Staff Development Council.

Stern, D. (1986). Compensation for teachers. *Review of Research in Education, 13*, 285-316.

Stiggins, R. J., & Duke, D. L. (1988). *The case for commitment to teacher growth: Research on teacher evaluation*. Albany: State University of New York Press.

Stringfield, S., Billig, S., & Davis, A. (1991). Implementing a research-based model of Chapter 1 program improvement. *Phi Delta Kappan, 72*, 600-606.

Thies-Sprinthall, L., & Sprinthall, N. A. (1987). Experienced teachers: Agents for revitalization and renewal as mentors and teacher educators. *Journal of Education, 169*, 65-69.

Toch, T. (1991). *In the name of excellence: The struggle to reform the nation's schools, why it's failing, and what should be done*. New York: Oxford University Press.

Tracy, S. J., & MacNaughton, R. (1993). *Assisting and assessing educational personnel*. Boston: Allyn & Bacon.

Warren, D. (1985). Learning from experience: History and teacher education. *Educational Researcher, 14*(10), 5-12.

Wilson, M. (1993). The search for teacher leaders. *Educational Leadership, 50*(6), 26.

Wood, B. (1980). You're the teacher, tell us what we're supposed to know: An andragogical dilemma. *Journal of Staff Development, 1*, 119-125.

Wood, F. (1989). Organizing and managing school-based staff development. In S. Caldwell (Ed.), *Staff development: A handbook of effective practices* (pp. 26-43). Oxford, OH: National Staff Development Council.

Wu, P. (1987). Teachers as staff developers: Research, opinions, and cautions. *Journal of Staff Development, 8*(1), 4-6.

Index

CORWIN
PRESS

The Corwin Press logo—a raven striding across an open book—represents the happy union of courage and learning. We are a professional-level publisher of books and journals for K–12 educators, and we are committed to creating and providing resources that embody these qualities. Corwin's motto is "Success for All Learners."

Printed in the United States
2504